THE MAEVE BINCHY
WRITERS' CLUB

The Maeve Binchy Writers' Club

Maeve Binchy

WITH CONTRIBUTIONS FROM

*Ivy Bannister, Carole Baron,
Chris Bohjalian, Paula Campbell, Norah Casey,
Jim Culleton, Gerald Dawe, Marian Keyes,
Ferdia Mac Anna, and Julie Parsons*

ANCHOR BOOKS
A Division of Random House, Inc.
New York

AN ANCHOR BOOKS ORIGINAL, MARCH 2010

Illustrations by Robyn Neild

Owing to limitations of space, acknowledgments to reprint previously
published material can be found on page 292.

Library of Congress Cataloging-in-Publication Data
Binchy, Maeve.
The Maeve Binchy Writers' Club / by Maeve Binchy.
p. cm.
ISBN 978-0-307-47385-1
1. Binchy, Maeve. 2. Fiction—Authorship. 3. Authorship. I. Title.
PR6052.I7728Z48 2010
823'.914—dc22
2009042249

Book design by Rebecca Aidlin

www.anchorbooks.com

Printed in the United States of America
10 9 8 7 6 5 4 3 2 1

CONTENTS

PREFACE

The Maeve Binchy Writers' Club has been designed to motivate and encourage aspiring writers, as well as to entertain Maeve Binchy fans the world over. The idea first came from a course that ran for twenty weeks at the National College of Ireland, and which aimed to help individuals start and finish a book.

Each week Maeve wrote the students a letter, containing tips and advice on the theme being discussed during the sessions. Then special guest speakers, including some of Ireland's foremost authors, as well as representatives from publishing houses and writers' agents, talked about specific areas of writing. Essentially the program was about the process of writing a book and the business of being a writer, rather than the craft of writing. Thus it allowed participants to transform an idea into a manuscript ready to be shown to a publisher.

This book comprises the original letters written by Maeve to the members of the Writers' Club, along with contributions from some of the guest speakers on the program as well as new pieces for the American edition. It is interspersed with blank pages so that the reader can make his or her own notes, or even start writing his or her own short story, poem, or novel.

As Maeve says, "Everyone is capable of telling a story." This book is the perfect place to start for any budding writer.

THE MAEVE BINCHY
WRITERS' CLUB

INTRODUCTION

This book is for you because you once said or even thought that you might like to be a writer. This is your special journal. I've got one, too, and we must make them work for us. The whole point of this book is to remind you that that is what we do.

We write. We tell stories. We may create poems, do research into some special area, come up with thrillers, turn out a comedy. But we write. We don't just talk about it.

A little while back we held a course in Dublin where over two hundred people turned up every week. They heard from agents, publishers, stage, television, and radio producers; they listened to fellow writers and critics and, in the end, they sat down and wrote their own books. Most of them finished their books, and many of them will be published. What really helped the people attending the course was the discovery that they were not alone. They were not the *only* people sitting staring at a blank screen wondering if they were mad to try to do this. They all shared the huge self-doubt that writers know only too well: Who'll want to read *my* take on things? Hasn't it all been said and done already?

So we decided to make a writers' journal, a book of advice but with a few blank pages, too. Those are your pages. This is what will make the book complete. You could also have your own separate notebook, so that you have plenty of space to write longer pieces.

Remember all those ideas or half ideas that flashed into your mind and just as suddenly flashed out again? Of course you do. Now they can't escape. There's no need to wonder anymore if you wrote them down on the back of your checkbook, on the top of an evening newspaper, or in the margin of the telephone directory. They will be here in this book.

Suppose you hear a conversation with something marvelous in it, then I advise you to write it down in this journal. A hint is to write nice and small so that you won't use the book up with big, loping writing.

One of the first things I'm going to write is a phrase I over-heard as two people passed by my window the other day, talking about a friend of theirs.

"Her feet aren't any use to her. . . . Not as feet, that is."

It makes you wonder what on earth they *are* useful as, and there's surely some story it can go into along the way.

If you listen well, you will have many more and probably better quotes for yourselves. You will look through them and realize that it would be positively criminal to waste them, and you will start writing straightaway.

Another thing that you might keep in the journal are details of competitions, prizes, or awards. Anything at all that would give you a deadline, a time frame, an urgency to get it finished rather than allowing yourself to drift on, year after year, saying you'll do it someday.

You might also use this book as a place to keep lists of contacts. Suppose someone tells you about a marvelous editor at some publisher, a friendly literary agent, a magazine dying for new writers. Where better to file this information than in your writers' journal?

If you've bought this book, or someone has given it to you as a gift, then that means you must be interested in writing. So let's not have that interest remain a pious wish. This is a nice little book. We mustn't waste it. It is not for shopping lists or trying out anagrams for crosswords. The commitment has been made: we now have a writers' journal in our possession.

Yours will be different from mine, but they will all be helpful if they are opened, written in, read, and heeded.

There are some pieces of my own deeply wise advice scattered throughout. You may already know that it's much easier to tell other people what to do than to do it yourself. So I can look back on my days as a schoolteacher and speak with a lofty sense of authority. The most important thing to realize is that *everyone* is capable of telling a story. It doesn't matter where we were born or how we grew up.

I was the first writer in my family; all my relations were grocers or lawyers. They read books by other people, but they thought it was a bit fancy to go and write them. Also, I was from a quiet suburb in Ireland, which is a small country. Who would want to read my stories? But the imagination has no limits. Wherever you are is interesting if you know where to look. Putting your name at the front of this book is your promise that you are going to take this book, and yourself, seriously. Well, seriously enough to do something about this sneaking belief that you can tell a story as well as the next person.

Study all the advice and suggestions, certainly, but don't forget your own input. It could even turn out that the blank pages, the ones that you write on, might become the best self-help book ever written. After all, this book will be nothing until you fill it with your thoughts, ideas, hopes, and plans.

Good luck to us all.

Maeve

WEEK 1

Getting Started

Writing is a bit like going on a diet: you should either tell everyone or no one. If you tell everyone, then you can never be seen feeding your face in public without appearing weak willed. So that's a way of reinforcing your decision, and some people find it helpful. It does mean that you're somehow obliged to lose the weight you had promised aloud, or indeed finish the book. Or you could go the other route, and tell nobody—just hug your secret to yourself. Get thin by stealth, write the book, then burst onto an unsuspecting world with your new shape or finished manuscript. But whichever way you do it, you will need discipline and some kind of plan.

Time doesn't appear from nowhere. You have to make time, and that means giving up something else. Regularly. Like sleep, for example, or drinking or playing poker, or watching television, or window-shopping, or just lounging about with your family. You don't have to give these things up completely, but you do have to release five hours a week. So think now where you are going to find them. I gave up a bit of sleep. I had a full-time job in London, a lot of commuting, a heavy social life, a fair bit of travel, so it seemed a good idea to get up at five a.m. three times a week. I hated it. Of course, I hated it. Who would like sitting at a dining table half-crazed and trying to type, when the rest of the world was sleeping peacefully? Who could enjoy trying to swallow another mug of black coffee in an attempt to open the eyes and focus on what had to be done? In my case what had to be done were ten pages a week, and it took fifty weeks. I could not find those five or six hours at any other time of the day. If I left it to the evening, I would be too tired; the weekends held too much temptation; I hadn't the courage to give up the day job; so the dawn seemed the best choice out of a bad bunch.

Now, you may be a night owl, or you may have Thursdays off, or quiet weekends, so no doubt you will choose something more suitable for your lifestyle. But you will also have a whole different set of excuses from mine. Like you may have children. So you have to work around them. They must sleep *some* of the time. You may have an unsupportive partner who claims that you are no fun if you are stuck into this book-writing thing. I think you could point out that there are 168 hours in the week, and that you will be great fun for 163 of them. If you want to find those five hours, you will.

A Few Hints

Keep all your writing things together: computer, laptop, paper, printer, notes, research—whatever. Not everyone is lucky enough to have a study or even a spare room. So what I used to do was keep everything on a trolley under the stairs and drag it out when it was needed. That way I avoided all the time-wasting business of assembling it each early morning.

Mark into your diary each week which hours you will spend on writing and how many pages you expect to get done. If you write that down, you will do pages thirty-four to forty-four, then you have no escape and it will stop you from sitting there staring at the wall. Accept no interruptions during your five hours: no phone calls, no answering doors, no requests from children to come and play. These are delightful distractions that you will feel that a Good, Proper Person should give in to, but you must be ruthless. There are ways around everything, including asking five friends or neighbors or elderly relatives to keep an eye on the children for one hour each.

Finally, listen carefully to all the good advice that follows. And even more important, follow it to the letter!

Good luck!

Maeve

WEEK 2

◦~◦

Writers' Groups

Writing can be very lonely, and you can get great attacks of self-doubt. So, in a way, it makes sense to bond with a group of like-minded people who have also set out on the same kind of journey. For one thing, it will stop you from thinking that you are the only person in the world mad enough to believe that there's a book in you, and for another, it means you will meet sympathetic people instead of dealing with those who think you are crazy and should be learning belly dancing or car maintenance instead. Let me give you some of my own personal views on the advantages and dangers of a writers' group.

There's a danger that it could become a talking shop. A place where everyone endures everyone else's work as a kind of payment for having them listen to yours—like golfers waiting patiently through the tales of other people's chipping and putting until they can tell their own story.

Then there's the advantage that you can hear the mistakes others make and learn from them. It's much easier to see the flaws in someone else's work than in your own. The man who drones on and on giving endless descriptions of the sunset might bring you back sharply to your own writing and make you examine it more carefully. Or the woman who has a cast of thousands of characters, confusing everybody . . . this could make you re-think a bit, too.

Another danger I see in writers' groups is that of overpoliteness. I know that I would be guilty of it, because if a fellow member were reading out the greatest load of rubbish with an eager, delighted face I just could not be sufficiently cruel as to say how bad it was. And then I'd be afraid that others were being similarly overpolite to me. Perhaps your group should have a policy on honesty.

A writers' group would have the great advantage of keeping you up to scratch, like Weight Watchers does, or Alcoholics Anonymous. If you have to turn up with something written every Wednesday, then it's easier to keep to your schedule than if you had to deal only with yourself. It's dead easy to make a convincing argument to yourself. We have all done it. "You're tired, Maeve; don't be so doctrinaire; you don't need to write *every* week," and so the slippery slope begins. It's harder to explain to a group that you were tired. They were all tired, but they did their writing.

Another danger of a writers' group is that it might make you feel inadequate. Suppose there are one or two confident writers in the group who are very good; it could send you back into your shell. Or worse, you might want to denigrate your own work and imitate them instead. This would be a pity, but I have heard of cases where it has happened. Anxious people compare themselves unfavorably with leading lights. They feel confirmed in their belief that they are no good and quit before it's really begun. Maybe they were always going to do so, but it's sad when the very vehicle of mutual support and encouragement that was supposed to help them actually just makes them too scared to really give it a go, and is somehow proof that they are right to opt out.

Despite these few dire warnings, I do believe that writers' groups can be a great power for good. I have a friend in England who went to a group, and they all hated one another's novels-in-progress but liked one another. They all gave up on the fiction writing and wrote a cookbook instead. They got it published, and four more in a series after it, and still meet every week and are firm friends. I suppose, like everything, it's up to you what you bring to and take from a writers' group. I hope that a lot of you may go that route and that you will be able to exchange information and constructive criticism. You probably have much more courage about being honest than cowards like myself. I think my problem was that for years I had a neighbor who used to say proudly, "I speak as I find." The thing was that she invariably found something unpleasant to speak of.

May it be very different for all of you!

WEEK 3

◡

Telling a Story

They say that when beginning a story you should always try to catch people at some interesting juncture of their lives, like when they have to make a choice or a decision, or when someone has betrayed them, or at the start of love or the end of love. It's better to come across them at some kind of crisis than in the middle of a long, lazy summer where nothing happens.

The notion of change is important in a story. It would be a dull tale indeed if the hero took no notice of the disintegration of his family, if he were the same unaltered dullard after four hundred pages. The reader would feel fairly shortchanged.

I can't tell you what story to write. Nobody can do that except you. But I can share with you some of the advice I got along the way from wise editors, men and women whose job it is to know what people like and to keep us writers somehow on the rails.

They told me that we must be *interested* in the hero or heroine—that doesn't mean making the person into a walking saint or goody-goody, but it does mean giving him or her a strong and memorable personality. There is no point whatsoever in spending pages and pages describing someone who is a dithering, dull kind of person without purpose, views, or motivation. Nobody will finish such a story. We have to care enough about the people to follow them through to the last page. When I first heard this, I began to panic a bit and asked humbly what kind of people might be interesting enough to hold the reader's attention. I wouldn't be able to create Captain Ahab, the man who pursued Moby-Dick, or Rhett Butler, who didn't give a damn. But I was told that writing wasn't a matter of painting by numbers. They couldn't just create some formula, leaving me to join up the dots. I had to *think*, and work out the kind of people whose lives and adventures I would be interested in myself. This way I might be on the way to making others interested in them, too.

In my case, I was interested in people who were told that if they were good they would be happy, and were therefore disappointed when it didn't always turn out for them. So I worked out that, in a way, people create their own happiness not just by being good, whatever that is, but by seeking opportunities, taking chances, taking charge of their own destinies. It interested me as a start and then kept me going. It could work for you, too, if you found a theory around which to base a story, but there's no point in anyone else telling you what to write about. You'll end up writing their ideas, not your own.

Another good piece of advice I got was to think of the story as a journey. Something happens to the main character at the start, and we follow him or her dealing with it, or not dealing with it, or ignoring it, or making it worse. Whatever. Now, I don't mean a literal journey; they don't even have to leave home. But they have to progress, be different people for better or worse at the end.

The man who thinks his wife is unfaithful, his son on hard drugs, his colleagues in the office on the take, or his own gambling is out of control has to do *something* to change the situation. You can't leave him static in the same plight at the end of chapter fourteen as he was at the outset. The woman who has a bad medical diagnosis, a faithless friend, an unjust accusation of shoplifting, or proof that her brother is a murderer must take steps of some sort over whatever it is. She can't sit there like a dumbo for page after page letting it all wash over her.

An editor will also stress that pace is important when you are telling a story. Again, nobody can hold your hand over this, but I have found that at the beginning it helps to make a kind of chart of the book chapter by chapter, giving myself orders like, "By the end of chapter two we must know that she cannot afford to pay the rent and will be evicted," and then, "By the end of chapter three we must know that her rent will be paid for her, but at a price." If you do this in advance it stops you from dawdling about till you're ready and generally dragging the thing out and making it endless. There's no right pace or wrong pace; it's up to you. But there's no harm in being aware of it. A gentle, lyrical story will call for one kind of speed, a fast-moving action thriller another.

I hope it's all going well for you and that you are getting your ten pages a week done, as I am myself despite a broken arm and a general wish to do anything rather than write.

But I told you it was easy, so I have to believe it, too.

Anyway, there's a sort of solidarity in numbers.

Maeve

WEEK 4

∽

Writing Short Stories

This week I had to write a short story for an anthology, and I thought the best help I could be to you is to share all the questions I asked myself and how I attempted to answer them. At the end of this book you will find a few new stories I have written.

Where to set it?

In my case this was easy. It has to be about Dublin, so I placed it in a small house on a Dublin street that used to be working-class but was moving upward in parts. This would mean I could have all sorts of neighbors if I needed them—but I remembered it's only a short story, so no time for a pile of neighbors.

When is it set?

I think this anthology is more for a younger readership, but then again almost everyone is younger than I am, so I decided to make it present-day and see it from the point of view of a restless fourteen-year-old who is dissatisfied with her parents and over-impressed by her stylish aunt who comes to visit.

What are the main dangers in a short story?

For me the biggest danger is overcrowding the story with too many people. No time, I kept telling myself, to bring in her schoolmates, her teachers. No time for all the neighbors and their problems, no space to talk about her two awful younger brothers. Instead, just mention the two insufferable boys as a horrible presence in the background.

Before you begin, what must you do?

You *must* know the end. Otherwise you are lost. I have begun far too many short stories that died the death because I didn't know where they were going. You don't have the luxury in a short story of not knowing how it will turn out and waiting until you see how the characters are getting on. I had to force myself to write down the resolution. What was going to happen to the girl's relationship with her aunt? Would the aunt guide her through the drama or be useless? Would the girl know the difference

between wise and crazy advice? I was tempted to start writing it and see how it went, but do this and you are sure to end up waffling.

Okay, so you know the end; how do you begin?

I think you open with the action, introduce the two main characters. I began with the girl waiting for the aunt's annual visit. I don't do much descriptive stuff at the start. If I were to tell you all about the house and the garden with bicycles in it, and the wallpaper and the shabby stair carpet, it might fill in the texture but I'd still be writing it a month later. Get them up and running and start moving them toward the end.

A lot of dialogue or not?

Enough to move the story on. The girl's mother could say something that shows us what a hard life she leads; the girl should say something that lets us know how vulnerable she is, and something else later showing us how she has moved on.

What kind of a time frame?

In this case, for my plot it had to take place over a period of two years. So if I am moving them on at that pace there's no time for long descriptions of what they had for breakfast, nor too much "he said" and "she said." I was tempted to follow the aunt as she went from one cultural event to the next, but if I *did* follow her the plot would never have taken place, and the aunt and the reader and I would still be stuck at some exhibition.

How long is a short story?

It's a bit like asking how long is a piece of string. In this case they didn't specify a length (it is actually easier when they do). Anyway, it was about 3,500 words. That's eight pages of my typing. It took one day to plan it out and four days to write, at about four hours each day.

Is it any good?

I have absolutely no idea. I vary in my thinking. Sometimes I look at it and believe that it's tender and sensitive; then I move on and the next day I truly think it's a load of rubbish and that editors of the anthology will return it in disgust.

But I'll tell you what it is . . . it's finished!

Maeve

- *Short stories are satisfying, complete pieces of fiction, and many writers use them to practice their art. But where do you start, how do you finish, and, most important, how do you make it the best it can be? Award-winning playwright and story writer Ivy Bannister's eight-point plan offers some excellent suggestions.*

Eight Steps to a Short Story

Ivy Bannister

1 *Identify your obsessions*   What interests you passionately? What is your brain constantly chewing over? Motorcar racing or breeding orchids? Harassment in the workplace? Stroppy teenagers? Your father? Whatever it is, that's your subject matter. It's easier to write about what fascinates you, and your enthusiasm will seduce your readers, too.

2 *Characters*   It's tough to do without them. You'll probably have a central character whose perspective shapes the narrative. Scribble down what you know about this character. Don't be shy. Have fun. The more you know, the more your story will flow.

3 *Focus*   A story needs a goal, a target, a climax. Or, more formally, a point at which your characters' lives are changed forever. Get some kind of idea of what this might be— however hazy—before plunging in. Why do you want to tell this particular story? What is its denouement?

4 *First draft*   So you've identified your subject, characters, and a target: now it's time to get started. Dump everything you have to tell onto the page as fast as you can, not bothering at this stage with polished sentences or choosing exactly the right word. Aim for your goal. When you get there, congratulate yourself. You now have the bones of your short story. That's the good news. The bad news is that the perspiration lies ahead—but not quite yet.

5 *Research*   In flinging out your first draft, you may have realized that there are holes in your narrative, things that you don't know. Now is the time to find out more about your characters and their world. Say, for example, you are writing a story about your mother. Make a list of the things she says, her disagreeable—or agreeable!—habits. Peek into her wardrobe and take notes. Or perhaps your story involves someone who breeds rabbits. Go to the library and find a children's book, preferably, about the subject (adult books are long and complicated—you want the basics, fast). The Internet can be helpful, too. But don't overdo it. The purpose of this research is to enrich your narrative, not to become an expert on the subject.

6 *Producing a polished draft*   This is the bit that separates the writers from the scribblers, and it takes a long time. Inch by inch, you develop your messy first draft into a flowing, coherent narrative in which every word earns its keep. Good stories are not written: they are rewritten.

7 *Editing*   When you think you've done the business, put your story aside for a couple of days. Then come back and tighten it. Cut a lot, because less is more. We all repeat ourselves in casual conversation, but you don't want to do that in a short story, or your readers will abandon you.

8 *Final draft*   You're now too close to your work to make the final touches, so go off and literally forget your story. Write another one! See the world! Come back with a cleansed palate, which will enable you to make yet another set of revisions, which will produce the fine-tuned, excellent story that has a chance in a hundred of being published.

Finally, enjoy! If you don't, your reader won't.

WEEK 5

The Writers' Agent

I once heard a writer say that finding an agent was as fraught and complicated as finding a spouse, and there's a lot of truth in that. If it works it's terrific; if it doesn't it's worrying and depressing and there's the feeling that one side might want to get out of it and the other doesn't.

In an agent–author relationship there's plenty of room for a minefield of misunderstanding. The agent thinks the author should be speedy in the writing and the rewriting, yet endlessly patient while waiting for responses and results. The author thinks that the agent should be back in twenty minutes with news that the Hungarian rights have been sold for a fortune. The agent hopes that the author will understand the frustrations of dealing with busy publishers, writing endless letters, arranging meetings, jogging editors to read the manuscripts they have sent them. The author assumes that the agent knows how vulnerable and foolish we feel as the hours and days crawl by with no word until the eventual humiliating news: "I'm afraid they've decided to pass on this one."

So do we need an agent at all? Is it all more trouble and angst than it's worth?

I asked this of Gail Hochman, president of the Association of

Authors' Representatives, who says, "A good agent is the author's best advocate on business matters as well as a help throughout the entire publication process." She considers herself a problem solver, saying, "After the deal is done, so many awkward situations can arise on both sides for the editor and for the author, and I can quietly mediate a solution that makes everyone happy."

I believe that we *do* need agents. Badly. And here are six reasons why:

1 Publishers listen more to agents than to us. An agent gets a track record of offering readable, saleable stuff, so the publishers will look at an agent's submission more favorably than at our tremulous, tentative offerings where they can almost smell the quivers of hope and fear in our submission letters.

2 An agent is like a broker who knows the right place to send a manuscript. We could waste months submitting to people who buy only poetry when we are trying to sell science fiction.

3 The publishers are inclined to respond more swiftly to agents than to us. They don't want to alienate agents; after all, even if they hate our manuscript, the agent could quite possibly be representing someone marvelous next week.

4 We haven't a clue about money, advances, rights, reversions, translations, remainders, reprints. Why should we? Our job is to write. Agents are more than welcome to their percentage in exchange for taking all that off our shoulders.

5 It's in the agent's interest for us to do well. Agents get a percentage of the advance money and royalties you get from the publisher. It can be 10 or 15 percent. Any sane agent would prefer to have a percentage of $20,000 rather than $500. An agent will talk us up rather than sell us short.

6 An agent can be our greatest ally. They can tell us when we are waffling; they can head us off at the pass before we go forever down a wrong track. *They* can say that the lead character has become a pain in the neck or that our coincidences are ludicrous. We will take it from them because we travel the same road together, sharing success or failure. Often we can take criticism from an agent more easily than from a loved one.

So how do you find one of these magic agents?

I asked an agent for her best advice and she said that you should do your homework. The Association of Authors' Representatives Web site (www .aaronline.org) will give you a list of agents by category. There is no use sending your mystery to an agent who specializes in romance. I hear that agents like a one- or two-page summary to prove that you have a plot, three chapters to prove that you can write, and the return postage to show that you realize most agents get fifty to a hundred manuscripts a week.

What will make your submission stand out?

If you have had *any* success in any relevant field, let the agent know. Perhaps you've had articles or a short story published before, or you actually work in a circus or on a deep-sea trawler, where the story is set. Whatever it is, tell the agent. And however gibbering you feel, try to sound confident. No agent wants to take on a bag of nerves; life is hard enough already.

Good luck in your trawl—after all, a lot of it *is* sheer luck, chance or coincidence as well as persistence.

Warmest wishes,

Maeve

WEEK 6

❧

Sustaining Progress

How much easier it is to write a bossy letter urging you to Sustain Progress and to Keep at It than to do these things myself! This morning I should be tackling chapter seven of something, in the sure and certain knowledge that chapter six was endless and droned on and on until it would drive anyone demented. All my confidence and enthusiasm about the story has gone; I would as soon go out and help the people drilling the street outside our hall door than get down to writing. So mercifully today I have an excuse . . . I have to write a letter to you.

But—and this is the big *but* that I want to share with you—I *will* go back to chapter seven this afternoon, because I have this notion of myself that I am reliable and I want to live up to it. I'll finish the damn thing even if it kills me. It's all a matter of discipline, I tell myself firmly, as if this will solve everything. Actually, I'm not at all disciplined, and despite my self-delusion I'm not even very reliable. This is just a myth I spread about myself. I heard myself saying yesterday on the phone, "The one thing I am is reliable," and I always believe it at the moment I'm saying it. I think it would be desperate if people said you were unreliable; it would be insinuating that you were dishonest. So that's what keeps me going. I promise to have it delivered by a certain day, and delivered it will be.

It used to be the case that, quite often, the last ten days before delivery involved being up most of the night. But I'm not able to do that anymore, so I have to motivate myself to keep at it on a fairly regular basis. In the next section, Norah Casey has some good advice for you about motivation, but I do it mainly by a series of threats and rewards. Idiotic as they sound, one of them might work for you.

1   If I get the first four pages of chapter seven done today and the action has moved on rather than stayed static, I will have a huge glass of chardonnay and read more of Christopher Plummer's autobiography.

2   If I don't get four pages done, I will sit down and make those three telephone calls that I have been putting off for weeks, because they will each involve grief and irritation.

3   A few weeks ago, I promised that if I got chapter five finished I'd go to see *The Roy Orbison Story* and be in an audience of mature people who remembered "Only the Lonely" and "Pretty Woman" from way back. I finished the chapter and it was just one terrific night out.

4   I said that if I had not managed to update the outline that was
    by now going very askew, then I wouldn't go out for a Chinese
    meal with six women friends. I sat at home stabbing at the
    machine while they apparently had the time of their lives and
    revealed all kinds of things about themselves, things that
    sadly I will now never know.

5   There are long-term treats, too. If I finish the whole book a
    week before the day it's due, I will book us a week in the
    country and spend hours rather than just minutes looking at
    the scenery and the faces of mountain goats and sheep.

6   If it's all a mad rush, as it has often been before, we won't go
    anywhere. Just torture ourselves with brochures and thoughts
    of what might have been.

Now, all this may seem appallingly self-indulgent and silly to
you, but I have to make up my own rules. So do you. And however glum we might all feel, we must remember that this is
where the losers give up. We will not be among them.

Warm wishes,

Maeve

- *There's a huge empty piece of paper looking up at you from your desk, or maybe it's a blank computer screen. But you're up against a deadline, or you've stolen an hour and a half to write, and nothing at all is coming. What do you do? Norah Casey, chief executive of Harmonia, Ireland's largest consumer and contract publishing house, shares her secrets on overcoming the problem of an empty brain.*

Maintaining Your Motivation to Write

Norah Casey

The most frightening experience in any writer's life is the dreaded "writer's block." The bleakest of spells, however, can be overcome with some tried and trusted techniques.

First, remember that most writers, even the very successful ones, have suffered from the condition. It is important to diagnose the problem honestly. Ask yourself if your inability to write is due to procrastination or a genuine block in your thought processes. All writers go through periods when motivation is in short supply, and what they suffer from is procrastination rather than true writer's block. Recognizing what you are up against and dealing with it is the first step toward getting yourself back to the computer screen. Procrastination is a symptom of many conditions. Stress, lack of energy and time are sometimes the underlying reasons. Many writers—particularly those starting out—have full-time jobs or are full-time homemakers. Finding space to write is the biggest challenge. One well-known writer got up at four-thirty every morning to fit in a few hours before the children woke; another used the time after they went to bed. Recognizing the limitations of your working day and making a plan to fit in your writing time is imperative.

Maintaining your motivation to write is equally important. Seasoned writers say that difficulties with maintaining enthusiasm can happen at any time, but often the most demotivating phase, when procrastination can really set in, is when you are working on a rewrite. Again, diagnosing the problem is the key to resolution. Revisiting why you wanted to write in the first place is often a good place to start. The discipline of writing will return only if you capture the enthusiasm and determination that set you on the road to writing that particular story or novel.

For some the motivation is financial—and there is nothing wrong in that. For others, the desire to see their name in print is the primary reason. However, neither of these spurs will sustain you on the long road to publication. More often, successful writers have an urge to communicate a story or an idea. They begin with tremendous self-belief in their ability to put their thoughts across through the medium of the written word. Even the mildest criticism in the early days of writing can be a significant setback—some may even decide to give up. Writers' groups, trusted colleagues, and loved ones are invaluable in helping to rebuild your confidence. As you become more expert at writing, your ability to withstand criticism will improve—to the point, perhaps, where you may even welcome tough critics into your life and learn to trust someone who will tell it how it is.

Some writers say that the strongest motivation often comes from the doubters around them. They remember a tutor, a friend, or a relation who put them down and belittled their attempts at writing. Proving someone wrong can be a strong determinant to succeeding as a writer—so remember their put-downs and reaffirm your vow to see them eat their words!

Whatever the reason for your procrastination, remember that there are always antidotes. If you are tired, then get some sleep and return when your energy levels are back up—you need to be rested and energized to write well. If you are plagued with self-doubt, read your work over again, call a friend, or join a group. Read what other writers have said about their own periods of insecurity—you will find you are in good company. Many writers throw themselves into housework to avoid getting down to work. Learn to ignore the dust and the washing-up and go straight to the computer—and don't surf the Net when you get there! Instead of putting the kettle on yet again, make a pact that you will have a cuppa after two hours of writing. If you are bored with writing, or if you find your thoughts straying and can't get yourself back into the plot, take time out and do something completely different. Go for a brisk walk rather than just turning on the radio or TV. Writing, like any job of work, improves with a disciplined regimen. Novice writers often find this difficult, especially when there is no one but themselves to enforce deadlines. Be your own boss and implement a punishment-and-reward system—set deadlines for yourself and treat yourself if you achieve them, and find something suitable as punishment if you don't!

The horror of staring at a blank screen with nothing, not a single thought transferring itself from brain to keyboard, is the most frightening experience for any writer. A true writer's block—not just a period of procrastination—can last from hours, to days, to weeks, months, and even, some writers say, for years. At the outset, that lonely struggle between you and the screen can be overwhelming. A genuine block is rarely due to short-term problems, but it is worth going through all of the reasons why your thought processes might have come to a full stop to see if there is a straightforward solution.

The most common reason for writer's block is problems with the story line. There are no hard and fast rules as to how to overcome this but, without swift attention, an acute attack can turn into a chronic condition. Start by revisiting the story line. Have you introduced new elements, and are the characters true to your original outline? (It is common to go off-track—sometimes it even improves the story line.) If you have veered from your original plan then you have to decide whether to rewrite the outline, and potentially the plotline of the story, or rewrite chapters. Both are painful decisions to make, but remember that writing is a work in progress, so revisiting your ideas is an essential element of writing successfully. By focusing on the bigger picture (the framework, context, plot, and characters), you will find the details often become clearer.

Many great writers emphasize the need to be simple and direct in your storytelling—write as you would talk. One of the really useful ways of getting over writer's block is to do just that—talk about the story and the problem you have come up against. Speak to friends, your writers' group, or even to yourself. Don't underestimate the value of "thinking time"—in the bath, on the bus, while you walk. You will solve the problem more quickly away from the screen. But don't be tempted to stay away too long. If you are really stuck, then write about something else for a while—try not to lose the discipline of writing as you work your way through it.

Whatever you do, don't give up. All writers go through periods of slumped starts, sagging middles, and empty endings, so be honest with yourself about why you are avoiding the screen. Don't call it writer's block unless it really is the full-blown variety. Stay focused on the bigger picture and remember why you decided to write in the first place. Make a list of distractions and keep it next to the computer as a constant reminder of what makes you give in. If you're going to be your own boss, remember that successful managers are firm, fair, and consistent—so make rules, deadlines, and work schedules and stick to them.

Above all else, enjoy it. Despite the hurdles, remember how privileged you are to have that great gift of writing.

WEEK 7

~

Finding Your Voice

I never knew what was meant by "finding your voice." Not for ages. But I think I know now. I believe it means finding a way to write that is comfortable for you. It's finding the method to tell your story that seems natural and unaffected. That way you're not going to get caught out all the time trying to keep up with some kind of style that you think may be appropriate.

We should think of Shaw's *Pygmalion / My Fair Lady*, in which the cockney girl can pronounce "the rain in Spain" perfectly, but comes totally unstuck in a moment of crisis. I know people in Ireland who have changed their accents considerably, and I have an unworthy wish to wake them in the middle of the night with the news that their house is on fire just to hear if they cry, "Jaysus," like the rest of us. I think that finding a voice in writing has everything to do with integrity and little to do with stylistic imitation. If we admire someone a lot, then it's tempting to think that if we, too, wrote like that we would be terrific. Not necessarily so—we could end up just looking like poor copies.

I adore William Trevor's writing; I would *love* to be able to create a relationship, a family, a community, a sense of tension as he does. But there's no point in trying to imitate him; I'd fall flat on my face. Instead, I read him with awe, and I wonder if there is any trick or writing technique he has that I might somehow "borrow." I have been to talks he has given and even asked questions from the audience, and I have learned a lot.

One thing he says is that if you have several characters and setups in a story, the trick is to move on fairly quickly from one to the other. If you are starting to get bored by a scene, you can be sure that the reader would be bored a page ago. Move on, he says, and it's great advice.

He also suggests leaving a short story in a drawer and not looking at it for six months. That, I am afraid, would be a total nonstarter for me. The moment I have "The End" written, the story is in an envelope or an e-mail to someone. But in a perfect world William Trevor may be right when he says that if you let a story settle for six months you can see all the mistakes as if they were highlighted in yellow Day-Glo. Yes, but suppose you saw the whole story highlighted? What would you do then?

The point of all this is: what do we get from other writers? My bossy advice is that you don't want to *copy* other writers; what you want is to "borrow" some of their techniques and present them in your own voice. It's no use asking any writer, "Where do you get your ideas?" Oddly, it's the question writers are asked most often, and it's almost impossible to answer in any way helpfully. You get your ideas by asking yourself what kind of situation you would be happy to sit down and write about every single week for seven or eight months. Usually it's something you feel comfortable with, like something from your own experience or from familiar territory. Or it could be something that fascinates you, for example, if you were interested in military history and were going to write a historical novel set at the Battle of the Bulge.

My most fervent suggestion is, don't allow yourself to believe that if a topic worked for one person it will work for you. That way you are denying yourself the real pleasure of writing, which is telling your own story in your own way. There are loads of hints out there, and I have always found writers are willing to share them rather than hug the secrets of success to themselves.

There will always be plenty of readers keen for things to read. Success is not a pie where everyone who gets a slice has somehow diminished what is left for everyone else. That's not really how it works. Success is more like a cairn, a heap of stones where the more each person gets, the more it adds to the general body of work out there. Other writers are there to encourage us, to be the living proof that those hours of "keeping at it" can pay off. If we can learn a little hint here and there from every writer we read, and even more especially, from every writer we meet, then we will do well.

Maeve

- *Novels don't happen without effort, and being a novelist requires dedication and tenacity as well as skill. Writers must be prepared to take time discovering their voice, and writing and rewriting until the prose shines. Bestselling author Marian Keyes shares her no-nonsense approach to the hard work that goes into producing a full-length work of fiction.*

The Road to Success

Marian Keyes

People often ask me for advice on writing a book; because I'm a published author they assume I'm in on some big secret. But the good news is that there's no big secret, and the bad news is that there's no big secret. The advice I give is very practical, and it's advice that people rarely want to hear. But I'm not holding out on you, honest to God—this is really how it's done. First, stop talking about it and sit down and start writing it—word by word. No one else can write your book but you. If you don't write it, it won't get written.

Second—and brace yourself for a cliché—writing really is 1 percent inspiration and 99 percent perspiration. Writing is *work*. Perfect characters, plots, and sentences don't spring fully formed from the mind of a writer onto his or her screen. They are achieved only by time, patience, thought, and constant rewriting.

Don't be surprised if your first efforts are shockingly bad— indeed, expect to marvel at the gap between what you want to say in your head and how it appears on the page. But persevere; chances are it will improve. Formally set aside time to write—

respect your book enough not to try to fit it in, in bitty gaps, around the rest of your life. This is advice that really seems to rankle—perhaps because there's an assumption that writing is somehow "magical," so that it almost does itself. But it doesn't. So be prepared to get up an hour earlier every morning, or miss out on your favorite TV show in the evenings, or Saturday afternoons around the shops; if you were learning to drive or speak a new language, you'd devote time to it. Better still, try to write at the same time every day—this seems to trigger the subconscious into readiness.

Beware of setting yourself up as the "new" Monica Ali or the "new" someone else: it's always cringingly obvious. Instead write in your own unique voice and be proud of it. Be honest and write for yourself, not for some perceived audience; nothing compromises the integrity of a book like the writer tailoring it in advance to please a certain market.

Write what you know—and if you don't know it, be prepared to research it. If you're not sure of your characters' milieu, your book will lack conviction.

Joining a writers' group is often a good idea; you get advice, feedback, support, and an incentive to have *something* written to read out every week.

A few final snippets:

Always have a notebook on your person in case inspiration strikes.

It's better if you have a sympathetic protagonist—readers are less likely to stick with a book if they don't like the main character(s).

No killing off your main characters at the end of the book.

And when your book is finally finished—get an agent! Please. This vastly improves your chances of getting a decent deal from a publisher.

Finally—enjoy it! If you enjoy writing your book, the chances are that people will enjoy reading it.

WEEK 8

The Writer's Journey

We get courage from other people's stories. We get consolation from the way they tell about failures, disappointments, and crises. It means that we are not alone. We aren't the *only* foolish, overambitious folk who have a drawer full of rejection slips. It's very comforting to know that the Dan Browns, Graham Greenes, and Danielle Steels of this world had to cope with exactly the same thing, and aren't we all pleased that *they* didn't give up?

Marian Keyes has given you inspiring advice with her characteristic good humor, so this should keep you going and help you feel you can do it, too. But then Marian goes home, and you go home, and there is bound to be that moment when you say, "It's all right for *her*; she's bright and funny and can write dialogue like a dream. It's different for *me*." Well, it is, of course; it's different for everyone. But that's the great thing. If it were the same for everyone then we'd all be writing the same book, over and over. But we each have different experiences to draw on, different hopes and dreams; we find humor in different places, and that's why the book has never died out despite all the predictions that it would. The movies would kill it, they said, then videos, then the computer. It hasn't happened.

Is it pretentious to regard your book as some kind of journey? I think not. We are different people when we finish a book. We have had to face ourselves, think about what matters to us and what doesn't. We have to face our own prejudices and attitudes. And maybe admit that we are more shallow or possibly more intense than we had thought when setting out. None of this is any harm.

I discovered when I started to write that I was much more of a moralist than I had believed myself to be. In my stories I always seemed to manage it that the good are rewarded and the bad are punished. I didn't know that was the way I felt about things, and I wasn't altogether pleased. It sounded a bit like a pantomime in which people cheer the hero and boo the villain. But then I decided that since this was obviously the way I felt I should examine it carefully and see if there was any merit in it. Eventually, I worked out that my characters should find their own salvation, that if people in my books created their own happiness then they *deserved* to be rewarded, and if they messed about and dithered then they deserved to fail. I was happy enough with that simple philosophy, and so it will be with you.

A book *is* a journey. Well, it is if you finish it. If you don't then it's no journey at all, just a series of stops and starts and eventual disappointments. I think that this might be the point in the journey when you pause and examine, for five minutes, the actual possibility that you *don't* finish the book. Only five minutes, mind you, not long enough to think about it as a real likelihood but enough to shake yourself up. If you stop now, let's look at what you have wasted. The time you spent on something you've now abandoned, all those nights when you could have been going to the cinema or for a meal with friends. You've lost the chance of getting to know yourself better. The feeling that you *did* it rather than just talked about it. The chance of saying to people, "Of course I finished it." The possibility of getting it published. The possibility that people might love it. The fact that it could have earned you money—had it been finished. You could have impressed and delighted your friends and family. You could have irritated and confounded your enemies. You wouldn't suddenly abandon a long-planned journey to somewhere just on a whim, would you? Of course not.

Your five minutes are over. You're not going to abandon this journey either.

Bon voyage!

Maeve

WEEK 9

⌒

Visualizing Success

It almost feels like tempting fate to visualize success. It's like saying to the gods that we know we are going to win when we have a sneaking feeling that the gods mightn't like such a cocky attitude and could easily dash us down. Yet I think it's important that we try to do it all the same. It's a powerful lever in keeping us at it, particularly on those days when *anything* seems more attractive than trying to get the ten pages done. So when reality kicks in asking us who the hell do we think we are, Hemingway? it's wiser not to listen to those voices. Better to choose the over-sunny way and ask yourself, Why *not* me?

When I had my first collection of short stories published back in the seventies, I realized that what had kept me going all the dark mornings when I got up at five-thirty to get three hours at the typewriter before going to work was the thought of the publication party. I could visualize it, and *did* visualize it every time I dragged myself out of bed and forced down hot black coffee to wake me up. I could see the people coming in the door of somewhere glittering. I could hear them murmuring of how good I was to have finished the collection and predicting great things for me. Vain, nonsensical, childish—yes, certainly, but it worked. It kept me at it.

Those were often sad, glum times to be an Irish journalist in London, with bombs, sieges, and hunger strikes to report. No wonder I kept looking forward to the publication party. When it happened, it wasn't at all what I had expected. For starters, the publisher nearly fainted when I started talking to him about whether we would have sausages or just cheese spread on biscuits. He hadn't intended to have any party at all. My face crumpled in a mighty disappointment. Why had I been getting up so early for months? I wondered. He couldn't help me there. So I decided to spend some of my advance on a party. It bought two hours in a room over a pub in Covent Garden, some red and white wine and crisps. But there were speeches and photographs and lots of pals there and some booksellers, and I generously invited the publisher, who cringed with the shame of it all, and, in the end, it was such a good scene that it fired me to sit down and write the next book.

I have a friend, a writer, who says that he visualized moving at ease with famous writers and that that was what kept him going. He could see himself going into restaurants and saying, "Hi, Jhumpa," or "How's it going, Dean?" And in the end he did get that for himself, to such an extent that he was buzzing around meeting and greeting so many famous names that he almost forgot to write his own books.

I knew a woman who broke up acrimoniously with the man she loved, and his last words to her were along the lines that she would never amount to anything. She dreamed of the day he would see her face all over the bookshops. And that day arrived. It didn't matter to her that much by then, but the visualizing had worked. I remember reading how Frederick Forsyth was sacked by the BBC and promised as he left Broadcasting House, "I'll show you." And he certainly did.

I was at a ceremony last week where a captain of industry told the audience that very little in this world was ever achieved by pessimism. He was talking about companies having to *believe* that they were succeeding, visualizing a successful outcome, and then they could all work toward that and would be more likely to achieve it. Now, I think he was really talking from the point of view of management rather than the worker bees. Yet as you get older and more mellow you see wisdom in the most unlikely places, and I think he had a point.

Love from,

Maeve

WEEK 10

∽

The Role of the Editor

Everyone has been busy telling you how it's all in your own hands and it's up to you and you alone whether you get a book finished or not. In a way, of course, that's a good thing. It takes away all the props and the excuses that we so easily rely on. If we firmly believe that we are the only ones who can do it, that there's no cavalry out there galloping to help us, then we are more likely to get it done. But if you have been working hard, and the book is on track, then relax a little, because today's thought is about a huge source of help: the editor. This is the man or woman at the publisher whose job it is to get the book into shape for you, for them, for everyone. Editors are amazing people. They don't usually write books themselves, but they know what's right and wrong with *your* writing. They should be listened to with great attention.

I'll tell you how editors have helped me, and maybe you will see the role they play. The man who edited my first book of short stories, *Central Line*, said that since this book was meant to be set in London's bed-sitter land it was odd that all the characters spoke with Irish accents. I truthfully didn't know what he was talking about; there wasn't a "begorrah" or a "Jaysus" to be found anywhere. But he pointed out that Irish people answer a question by half repeating the question. "Are you going to take the children to the shops?" "Yes, I'm going to take them up to the precinct." The English would answer the question by saying yes or no.

So we went through the whole book, this editor and myself, anglicizing any of the characters who needed it, and it was much better in the end, mainly because you knew who was speaking. Later, when I had written my first novel, another editor went through it and said there was hardly a personal description of *any* of the characters! The reader had no idea what they looked like. I fought that for a little while, saying that I never really remembered much in real life what people looked like, were they fat or thin, blond or dark. I only remembered if I liked them or didn't. Politely she told me that I was the one who was out of step here, and could I try to think of them as missing persons where we needed a description in order to find them. And I was glad of that help, too.

Nobody in the world likes criticism. It's not human to smile in delight when someone tells you that a character you have slaved over turns out to be a pain in the neck. That happened to me when I invented what I thought was a delightful person—Sister Madeleine in *The Glass Lake*. She was meant to be a wise, watchful hermit who knew the town's secrets. The editor said she was sickening because she was always right. I bleated in her defense for a while, but the editor begged me to believe that she would drive everyone mad. I muttered unworthy thoughts (only to myself), like if she knew so much about books why didn't she write her own? But fortunately, I kept these thoughts to myself, and made the changes. Like I made Sister Madeleine responsible for a poor little blind kitten getting drowned. Is that all right, editor? Happy now? And of course she was right, and I'm very grateful. And so I learned to listen well to editors along the way.

There are many good reasons why you should learn to respect a good editor. They are like a second line of defense. You know how nervous and unsure we are anyway; well, if the editor thinks it's okay then that's someone on your side from the outset. And not only just someone; it's a professional. An editor would not be paid a salary by publishers if he or she just came up with turkeys and failures time after time. They know what works and what doesn't. Well, mainly they do. Sometimes they get it wrong. And they are just as afraid of having a loser on their hands as you are of being that loser. They are not the enemy. We play on the same team.

Just as it is with agents, it's easy to come across an editor whose manner grates with yours. My advice is to get over that feeling fast. You don't have to be the editor's best friend socially, only a professional colleague. Do your rewrites with a good grace or move on to someone else. But don't shoot yourself in the foot over some petty row. Your editor is your best ally in the publishing house. He or she will fight in your corner at meetings and conferences, saying you should have a good cover, a decent promotion budget, maybe even a book party.

Editors are much more likely to be right about things, like our droning on endlessly or being too flippant or shallow or whatever, than our own nearest and dearest. Once you have gotten as far as having an editor, you're in the home stretch. Handle editors courteously and with velvet gloves and listen to every word they say.

Meanwhile, congratulations to you all for sticking at it!

Love from,

Maeve

• Like accountancy or shopkeeping or picture framing, publishing is a business. Although it can be a mystery to aspiring authors, understanding how publishers work is essential if you want to find the right one for you. Carole Baron, my American editor, explains the editor's job.

To Be an Editor

~

Carole Baron

People often ask: What does an editor do? My answer is everything. And anything. (I will not, however, write a book based on a "concept" that was recently proposed to me by someone I know who feels he has a story that everyone wants to read. Chances are no one wants to read it, and I am not a writer; I am an editor.) My role as an editor ranges from choosing the book for publication to bringing it to the reader and everything in between. An editor is kept very busy by doing any one or all of the following things, and maybe even something that is not listed here.

1 Choosing the book.

2 Negotiating the deal with the author or agent.

3 Editing the book.

4 Working with copy editing, design, and production.

5 Writing jacket copy and catalog copy; working with the art director on the jacket.

6 Positioning the book within the company and being its advocate with sales and marketing.

7 Being aware of what is happening in the publishing business so you can make informed decisions.

8 Communicating to the author and agent what is happening to the book all along the way.

9 When the book is published, cheering for the good reviews and commiserating for the bad ones (and explaining that even Jane Austen and Herman Melville got bad reviews).

10 Being there for the author's next book.

Different editors and different publishing houses will work with you differently.

Some editors are acquisition editors: they are the rainmakers who go out to lunch, read the literary magazines for new authors, read the newspapers for ideas, trawl the Internet for what's hot. They are the ones who bring in the books. No one works alone. All publishing houses are different, but when an editor finds a book that he or she wants, no doubt there will be consultation with the publisher, the editor in chief, and in some cases the sales and marketing departments. A value is determined by how many copies the book might sell and how much advance against a royalty the author will get. After the terms are settled, a deal is made. The author is happy, the editor is happy. Sometimes the book is turned over to a working editor. Other times the same person who buys the book will edit the book.

Most nonfiction books are bought on proposal. And there is usually an ongoing discussion during the writing of the book, and while the work is in progress, portions of it will be sent to the editor to read and comment on. Most novels, especially first novels, are finished when they are submitted to the editor, so work can begin immediately. In second novels, the writer often talks to the editor before beginning the book, so everyone is in sync, and an outline or a proposal will be developed. The author may send in pages to the editor as he or she is writing. Other writers like to wait until they have a full first draft. The editor's job is to provide an atmosphere in which the author can do his or her best work. And the editor must adjust to the author's needs. Waiting for the next book can take patience and knowing when to ask, "How are things?" and when to keep quiet. I once worked with an author and I could never ask about progress, but I did put a fax machine (it was in the old days) in my kitchen so the pages would come in privately to me until the author was finished and ready to go public.

What does an editor actually do when the manuscript is "finished"? My job as an editor is to make sure the book is what the author wants and means. Sometimes the author is so close to a book that he or she needs someone to say, "I think you said this already." Or, in a recent novel I edited, I didn't understand why the main character was going home in the middle of a critical moment in her life. It just didn't make sense. Sometimes the author just assumes the reader will know, but in this case she thought she had already told us.

I also read the book to make sure the story is told in a narrative that moves forward. I read the book more than once, and if I feel a "clang"—something like I would imagine a musical conductor hears when, in the middle of the overture, one of the instruments in the orchestra strikes a wrong note—I go back and try to figure out why I heard that "clang." It may mean a small edit in a sentence. A word that is used isn't quite right. And there are times that a word is simply wrong. One writer I know sprang the sentence: "They coagulated around the piano to sing." This could be the symptom of relying on the thesaurus for words, and it was before the spell-check and thesaurus function on our computers so the substitution for "congregated" was not a computer error. Often the writer simply needs to transpose a paragraph or two to keep the chronology of the story in order. You can't have a character talking to his girlfriend until he actually gets in the room with her. Believe me, I have seen that happen.

Sometimes I read the manuscript and there is a gigantic "clang" and I can't figure out why. It drives me crazy thinking about it. So to break into my thoughts, I will start to outline the book. Yes, outline fiction . . . just to see the dynamic or the balance of the book. More often than not, midway through the outline, the air clears and I know what the "clang" is and can discuss with the author how and why I got there and what might be done to fix it.

Often, especially in first novels, the writer likes to put in everything she or he ever thought of or knows. It is a moment for the writer to show off, spill his guts, or simply go on about something that has nothing to do with the story. I call that the "kitchen sink" novel. Everything but the kitchen sink is put into the work. Getting the right stuff out is often a struggle with a writer. But believe me, it is most often the best thing to do. I once told a writer to simply get rid of the first chapter and start the book with the second chapter. Thank goodness the book went on to be a bestseller without that offending first chapter.

Editing nonfiction is quite different, but the editor's goal is still the same. Making sure that what the author wants to say is on the page. Making sure the topic is covered. In narrative nonfiction, many of the same rules apply as they do in fiction. In self-help books, there is a certain style used to get across the information, and usually in the voice of the author, who is no doubt an expert on the subject. Editing memoirs is a delicate balance of making sure there isn't too much or insufficient information for the reader to stay with the story.

When I work with a writer, I find a combination of telephone conversations, some e-mail dialogues, and then a follow-up with an editorial letter is the best way to go about it. That way, the editing becomes a conversation long before I sit down to do detailed notes. I ask questions to understand what the writer intends in those places where I am confused or stalled. Then I apply these conversations to the manuscript and write detailed page-for-page notes that indicate where the author needs to write or delete scenes, query word choice both in narrative and in dialogue, point out repetition of words and echoes of ideas, suggest "show, don't tell," and even suggest deleting a sentence or two because it just doesn't work.

There are some writers who want to go over the queries face to face with the editor. Not only is that geographically difficult, but I think it is better for the writer to have time to digest what I have to say before responding. So I usually mark up a manuscript, provide an overall note about the work and some editorial ideas, and then have a page-for-page letter. This way the author can take the time to read the notes without my breathing down his or her neck for a response. No one likes criticism, even if it is from a trusted editor, so this way the writer can read the note, think about the queries, and then discuss them. That is a lot better than a quick response that would be something like, "You are stupid. I am not making any changes."

Then we can talk about the comments, and often in the discussion, new ideas will come out. Just because there is a "clang" in one part doesn't mean that is the problem. Maybe setting something up earlier will eliminate the "clang" later.

But the best part for me is getting the revised manuscript back from a writer and seeing what has been done. If I had a problem with an action and expressed it and made suggestions on how to fix it, the most thrilling part is to have the writer think of something I never would have thought of in a million years but that makes the book, the story, the chapter, so much better. That's the real process.

Each book is different; every editorial approach is different. But in all cases it comes down to trust: that the editor wants the best possible book, a book that the writer envisioned and set out to write, and the author trusts the editor to get the writer to that point. Working with an editor is a two-way street for most writers; one writer said working with her editor was like "dancing with Fred Astaire."

When the editing is finished, the editor's job is not yet done. As you can see from the list above, there are lots of things to keep an editor busy in order to make sure the book gets the best possible introduction to its audience.

WEEK 11

∿

The Writer as a Journalist

I was a schoolteacher from the age of twenty-one to twenty-seven. I had written a few travel articles because in those days (1961–1967) people didn't go abroad as much as they do now, and it was easier then to sell a story about a summer in Greece, working at a U.S. summer camp, or plucking chickens in an Israeli kibbutz. Then, when I was twenty-eight, I got a job at the *Irish Times*, running the women's page, and for five years I wrote and organized features. Then I went to write features in London for twenty years. It was the most wonderful training and education, and I am very happy to share with you what I learned during that time. You can read some of my columns at the end of this book.

Urgency

When you write for a newspaper, everything is very urgent; it has to be written today and read tomorrow. This is hugely useful to us writers because it doesn't give us time to dither. And this is a great help. If you *have* to write six hundred words about Ladies' Day at the horse show or the Rose of Tralee festival, then you'll do it. Otherwise you'll be sacked. Journalism means that you can never indulge in the luxury of writer's block. The thought of a blank white column appearing in a newspaper is not one that can be considered, so however uninspired we might feel, we *write* the damn thing. Journalists often say to one another, "Don't get it right; get it written," and this is not such a bad rule in any kind of writing. You can always go back and change it later if you think it could be improved, but at least it's done.

Observation

If, as a journalist, you were to do a "color" piece, it meant you had to become very observant, and this was good training, too. You have to compete with television, and if you are describing something like the visit of Bill Clinton or the opening of the Olympics, then you know that 90 percent of your readers have seen it already on the TV. You have to rake the place with gimlet eyes, trying to find something that might not be immediately obvious. It's stood me in good stead over the years; I'm always trying to see something a little different in a situation, something that would make it stand out.

Learning What People Want

Newspapers are in daily competition with one another. They are desperate to wrench readers away from all the rest, so they are a good place to learn and understand what readers might want. There's a difference, of course, between knowing what they want and being able to deliver it! But I did learn from letters of abuse and letters of praise what pleased people and what annoyed them. They liked to be stretched a bit but not too much. They liked some of their old ideas challenged but not too radically. If we had known the expression then, we would have said they didn't like writers to be too much "in their face." So I suppose I learned what was to be my kind of writing then, as a journalist. Not too challenging, not hugely groundbreaking but giving them something that was within their own experience, something they could share. Ireland has changed so much since I started that it's a different world now. You will find different things in journalism to help and encourage you, so keep reading the papers and learn from the journalists whom you admire. And if you are ever running out of ideas, newspapers are filled with them. You'll be weighed down with ideas after reading a paper thoroughly.

Can You Join In?

It's the same old story. You have to banish the fear of rejection in order to try to write things for papers or magazines. There must be some area of expertise that you have—girls' soccer, Esperanto— can you share it with people in a nonhectoring, nonlecturing way? There are training courses in journalism you could inquire about, or you could ask to review books. Of course, they might say no, but by now you will have realized that the attractive physical attributes we writers have to develop are a thick skin and a brass neck.

And so, armed with these, let us cheerfully continue our writing journey.

Love from,

Maeve

WEEK 12

~

Writing for the Internet

When I was training to be a teacher we had a wise professor who said we should always tell the students that they shouldn't do as we do; they should do as we say. It may sound a bit bossy, but it suits today's theme. I know *nothing* about blogging. I would love to pretend that it is one of my great interests and skills, but you would find me out in thirty seconds. Yes, I do have a Web site at www.maevebinchy.com, and it gets updated every now and then, but I leave the technical side to experts. I am from the generation that did not find friends on Facebook, treasures on Twitter, or brilliance in blogs. I have never bought or sold anything on eBay, and my next year's resolution is "Not to Fear the Internet." I am so worried that all the chapters of books I have written will disappear if I touch any unfamiliar button that I err on the side of great caution.

But you don't have to listen to me telling you about my anxieties—instead you have Chris Bohjalian to set you right. He is not afraid of the Web or of cyberspace. And neither will you be. It's not just a matter of age or generation. Some seriously older people have mastered it perfectly. What Chris has to tell you about linking your blog makes great sense. The more ways you can lead people to what you do, the better. In real life we authors go around bookstores putting our works to the front; in cyberspace you must make it equally easy for people to find you. I also agree so much when he says you must be ethical and put in a blog only what you would stand behind if it were in a newspaper column.

Once upon a time, when I was young, a kindly nun at school said that all the words that were ever spoken were out there in the atmosphere, and wasn't that wonderful?

We looked at her, startled. Why would it be wonderful?

"Because we might hear our Lord's words, and the words of the prophets and the saints," she said simply.

As teenagers sitting in lines at school, we feared that the cruel or foolish or rebellious things we might have once said could be brought back. This was not good news. So I think you might remember this when you come to write a blog. From my limited understanding of it all, a blog lasts forever. It's worth considering. I most definitely would not like to read my views about a girl called Rosemary, who snatched the love of my eighteen-year-old life from under my eyes, half a century later! Nor would I like anyone to know that a warm, generous person like myself was capable of such hatred! Not that I can really remember what the love object and the hateful Rosemary even looked like.

Good luck with your blogging, and if resolutions are kept I may well join you next year.

Love from,

Maeve

- *The easiest way to begin writing for the Internet is to start your own blog. You can do this for free, and you can write about anything that interests you. Chris Bohjalian, author of eleven novels, including five* New York Times *bestsellers; maintains a successful blog on his Web site. Here he answers a few questions about blogging.*

Writing for the Internet

&#8e;

Chris Bohjalian

How often should a blog be updated?

I update my blog at least once a week, although I have friends who update their blogs almost daily. But a weekly schedule works for me, because I have written a weekly column for the *Burlington Free Press* since 1992. That means both that I am conditioned to write something new weekly and I have new material to add to the blog at least every seventh day. (Incidentally, my seventeen and a half years as a columnist have resulted in over nine hundred columns . . . or 607,000 words . . . or the equivalent of six novels.)

But you don't need to devote your online writing exclusively to blogging. You can also write smaller items on Facebook and Twitter. I update my Facebook status daily and add something to Twitter often two and three times a day.

A blog needs to be updated with sufficient frequency and regularity to keep readers interested. And that depends both on the whims of the writer and, yes, on the blog's subject matter. My friends who have political or news blogs sometimes have to update theirs two and three times a day when (for example) a state legislature is in session or there is breaking news.

My blog tends to be about friends and family and my cats' mistaken belief that Turd Hockey should be an Olympic sport, and so once or twice a week is plenty in my case.

When you sit down to write a blog entry, what is different about your approach than when you sit down to write a novel?

First of all, my blog is always nonfiction. It began with a newspaper column, so everything in it is true. The people are real, the quotes are real, the anecdotes are real. Nothing is made up. My novels, though grounded in research and conceivability, are fiction. Almost everything is made up. That's a pretty big difference right there.

Second, my blog—and my newspaper column—is meant to be read by a reader in one three-to-five-minute sitting. It's a very brief story. I like to believe people spend more than three to five minutes on a novel, though I know asking for a long-term commitment from a reader in the digital age is asking a lot.

Finally, I do live with the delusion that a novel is more timeless than a blog entry. Again, a few years ago, when I simply wrote my column for the newspaper, I knew that a few hours after the paper came out my column was likely to be starting a fire in a woodstove or lining a birdcage. The reality, of course, is that in the digital age a blog can have precisely the same longevity as a novel. They both exist on the Web for as long as there is such a network.

Is it like writing a newspaper column?

It is. The principal difference is that my newspaper column must always be precisely nineteen column inches or roughly 675 words. A blog entry can be dramatically longer or shorter. It can be a tweet or the length of a magazine essay.

How can you get people to notice your blog?

Links. I always have at least four or five links in a blog entry. I also flag new blog entries on the home page of my Web site, on Facebook, and on Twitter.

Is there anything you should never do on a blog?

I subscribe to the same code of ethics as a blogger as I do as a newspaper journalist. If I wouldn't write it for a newspaper, I won't write it in my blog.

WEEK 13

~~~

Tackling Men's Fiction

This is a whole new world for those of us who are not male. There's some way in, some code, and I certainly don't know it myself. Way back long ago, Jane Austen said that one doesn't write about what gentlemen converse about with one another, since one has no idea what they *do* converse about. Nothing has much changed since Jane's day, except that we know she was right. There have been books written saying men are from Mars, women are from Venus. Questions have been asked seriously about why men never ask for directions and women can't read maps. It is accepted that men have ways of communicating that women don't understand; there is some kind of system out there that they have the antennae for. I've seen it in action, but that doesn't mean I could write about it satisfactorily.

Women do like to talk about their feelings and emotions, and to me that seems easy and natural, but I'm nervous of writing about one-to-one intense conversations between men, in case I get them wrong.

Some authors appeal mainly to men: Tom Clancy, Len Deighton, Jack Higgins, D. W. Griffith, Frederick Forsyth, Clive Cussler, Lee Child, Gerald Seymour. This is neither praise nor blame; it's just a fact. I don't think there's a school of writing that's classified as Boys' Lit, not yet. But it may be the next big thing.

These are five points that come to my mind about writing for men, but check them out with the men in your writers' groups. Let this be the time when the women do all the asking and the listening. The only way we have of knowing whether we are getting things right is to go to the source.

1 *Men like information*   I gather this from reading all the authors listed above. They have genuinely inquiring minds that delight in things like how to assemble a Kalashnikov rifle, the exact pecking order in the CIA, the way to fix a poker game, or how to track some kind of wild animal. Women usually prefer to know why someone succeeds or fails, how to get someone who has stopped loving you to start again, or how to juggle work and home life. Maybe men like their fiction souped up with facts, and regard too much emotion and wondering *why* people said what they did or behaved as they did dangerously like those tedious, draining discussions at home with their wives.

2 *Men like excitement*   If you look at the subject matter of many very popular male novels you'll see that they are often set in

times of war, in high-office drama, in espionage, at the stock exchange, or in a munitions factory. Men don't seem to relish familiar, easily identifiable situations such as the domestic hearth. They like action moving fairly sharply against an exciting backdrop. They don't buy into long conversations about the family, the love affair, the betrayal, or whatever.

3 *Men like heroes and heroines to be lookers*   They don't want the action held up while a central figure worries about her facial hair, her drooping boobs, or while he broods about his thinning crown, or his insecurity with the opposite sex. Men like the cast to come with a full set of parts looking fine and even a bit glossy, admitting to no inadequacies. Remember James Bond when writing for males—they love his immaculate, stylish gear, and snobbish social habits.

4 *Men like shorter books*   If you don't believe me, go into a bookshop and check. Where are the blockbuster six-hundred-page tomes for lads? Where, indeed? Maybe they are busier than we are, or maybe they *think* they are. Maybe they read and have to read more nonfiction. Anyway, whatever the reason, if you're writing for fellas, write more succinctly.

5 *There are exceptions*   Of course, there are. Men loved *Bridget Jones's Diary*, because they thought it gave them an entrée to the confused mind of a woman. And both men and women can't wait for the new James Patterson, John Grisham, or Harlan Coben. This is not a gender war, a competition of stereotypes. It's not about which side writes better; it's about a genuine attempt to understand.

My warmest wishes to you all.

Maeve

WEEK 14

◡

The Publisher

When we get rejections, and almost everyone does, the tendency is to regard publishers as the enemy. This is counterproductive. The publisher is our great ally, and the bridge between us and the general public who will read our books. There's a sentimental expression in the United States that says, "Strangers are just friends you haven't met yet," but that's the way I always try to think about publishers. It stops you from getting enraged with them, and jealous of those who have succeeded where you have failed. I never found rage and envy good weapons on the admittedly tough road to getting published. I always preferred cockeyed optimism and insane good humor myself, and since it worked out all right for me in the end, I'm inclined to recommend it as a way to go. But within that hugely positive framework, there are some practicalities that you can all develop and expand on.

1 *Submitting your manuscript*

It is still best to send a preliminary letter, a one-page summary, and two to three chapters rather than the whole book; then if they like the look of it, they can ask you to send the whole thing.

You should leave wide margins and type in double spacing. No staples—they hate those and it tears the pages. Some publishers prefer it not to be bound, since they want to turn the pages. (Yes, I know these are slightly nitpicking considerations, but there's no point in irritating them before they've even read the first line.)

2   *Send the postage*

Again, it looks trivial, but put yourself in their place. Suppose they get a hundred manuscripts a week, most of which need to be returned. You can see how this would mount up. And you *are* asking them for a favor—to read and judge *your* writing. I have always believed that we writers should just assume that we pay the return postage. It doesn't look overhumble; it looks courteous.

3   *How soon should they reply?*

I've asked around about this, and the average answer is that we should reasonably expect to hear from a publisher within two months. I know it seems like an eternity to us. Sixty whole long days of watching the mail. But publishers have to send it out to their readers and wait for reports, or get it read in-house.

4   *Keep a copy*

Of course, nowadays with computers it's fairly hard to lose your entire year's work. In my youth people were always leaving three

hundred pages in a taxi or the ladies' loo or somewhere and never finding them again. I really do know someone whose brief-case disappeared with his whole novel in it, and we honestly never totally believed him. There was a lingering belief that the poor fellow was lying to us and it had never been finished at all. But wait. A year later it turned up in the locker of a man who had been a year abroad and had packed it into his locker before he left, thinking it was his. And we all spent the rest of our lives being apologetic and feeling guilty.

That couldn't happen now, but what might happen is that we could lose our corrections, rewrites, or alterations. So be sure to keep those as well.

5   *Publishers know the market*

We must always respect publishers as businesspeople. They know what sells and what doesn't. It's their business to know. Otherwise they wouldn't have offices and payrolls and backlists and a yearly publishing schedule. Of course, they may get it wrong sometimes—everyone does—but we don't want to dwell on that. It's only yet another anxiety to add to our growing col-lection. Instead, it's better to accept that they put their money where their mouths are. They take a risk on us every time. And because they see so many manuscripts and are in heavy competition with other publishing companies, they are sharper than we are about what will work and what won't. If I write a novel about some topic, like a rags-to-riches story based on a wronged woman who swore revenge on the rich family that scorned her, I might not know that there are already ten or twelve books on this theme out there and the market won't take another. But the publishers will know—that's their business, and we need them desperately.

Love from,

Maeve

- *It may be a cliché, but there's little doubt that once the hard work of producing your novel is over, there is still a huge job to be done to get it published. And once the contract has been signed, it usually takes a year before your precious manuscript becomes a physical book. Paula Campbell is publisher of Poolbeg, a publishing house based in Ireland, but the experience is the same on both sides of the Atlantic, although submitting manuscripts directly to the publisher rather than using an agent seems more the norm. She explains the best way to approach an editor—and the process that follows that magical moment when the publisher says yes.*

The Publisher

Paula Campbell

Sample letter

Dear Mr. or Mrs. Publisher,

I am not sure if fiction is part of your publishing program; nevertheless I decided to throw a few chapters in the post to you because I am confident that I have a huge bestseller on my hands, something along the lines of Dan Brown meets Maeve Binchy. My family and close friends all agree with me.

I just started writing over the last fortnight and I have found it remarkably easy. I have not enclosed a synopsis or further outline, as I am not entirely sure how the story or characters are going to develop, but I feel you will get a good idea from the material enclosed, and I am confident that I will be able to finish the novel very quickly. I generally write during the ad breaks on television.

I thought the handwritten style of the manuscript captured some of my bubbly personality, which would be good for publicity appearances on the telly. Please ignore the teeth marks on the corners—had a bit of a tug-of-war with my dog, who is a little possessive of my work but is my number one fan. I did not enclose an SASE because I know that you won't be sending this back to me! I am happy to allow you exclusivity for forty-eight hours; otherwise you will have missed a huge opportunity and I will be targeting other publishers.

Regards,

The Next Big Thing

The Role of the Publisher

Obviously, this is not the best way to approach a publishing house (your potential business partner) with a manuscript. As publisher at Poolbeg, I can receive up to two thousand manuscripts a year and publish only fifty—so that is a lot of rejections! While the gift of writing is something to treasure, you must approach it in a serious way. The publisher's decision to buy someone's book, assuming the material is appropriate to their list, is based on a combination of many elements, including a strong story, good writing, and well-presented material. So do your homework. Find out the guidelines for submitting manuscripts for each appropriate publisher and follow them. Send in the best work you can—and then be patient. It is not a good idea to threaten the publisher, who is, after all, your first point of contact! You just never know who could be on the way to making your dream come true. Using a literary agent will help you avoid many potential problems.

If you do get *the* call (which is one of the nice jobs of being a publisher, I might add) and the publisher wants to take on your work, the next stage is the signing of the contract. This may vary from publisher to publisher, but in general it will give you a lot of important information regarding finances, rights, and publishing time lines. Now the process really begins, and you will soon see that publishers work very far in advance, putting together plans as to when and how to publish the book.

About twelve months before the publication date the editorial process will start. Editor and author work together on getting the manuscript ready for typesetting, proofing, and ultimately into print—seeing the book on the shelf for the first time is a moment to savor!

During that time your book will also be the topic of many publishing meetings with the production, sales, and marketing departments, where we discuss:

The Best Publication Date

Taking into account seasonal factors, competition, and key bookshop activity, the publication date can be up to eighteen months after the contract is signed.

The Format of the Book

That is, do we publish in paperback or hardcover? Take a look in a bookshop and see the different shapes and sizes of the books; they will all have been discussed and planned at length.

The Cover

It is said, "Never judge a book by its cover," but that is exactly how many consumers make their choice, especially if it is a first-time author. The cover must tell the reader something about the story, indicate the target audience, and, ultimately, jump off the shelves and say, "Buy me"—a tall order sometimes! The area of cover design is a fascinating and ever-changing one.

The Sales and Marketing Campaigns

These are a vital part of the book's success, and the sky's the limit regarding creative, fun, and innovative ideas. We can loosely split this area into two: the sell-in and the sell-out.

The Sell-in—Getting the Book into the Bookshops

Booksellers buy new titles about six months in advance. They make their decision based on the cover and what the publisher plans in terms of marketing, advertising, and publicity, so most of the time they won't have read the book!

The sales reps are armed with the cover and campaign details and maybe the odd treat or incentive that lends itself to the book. For example, when Poolbeg published *Watermelon*, Marian Keyes's debut novel, a special consignment of gift-wrapped watermelons was delivered to each bookshop—which certainly made a lasting impression. Chocolates and champagne are also popular for some reason!

The Sell-out

This is what needs to be done to get the finished books from the shops out to the consumer in terms of bookshop promotions, posters, displays, author events, advertising, and, of course, publicity.

A special note about publicity: no matter how good a book is, despite the publisher's best efforts, they cannot guarantee that a book will be featured on television or reviewed in daily papers. The area of commercial fiction in particular is crowded and competitive, with an estimated fifty thousand books published annually, so the competition for coverage is fierce and the media are always on the lookout for that exclusive angle. Sadly, writing a book is just not enough.

I hope that gives you some brief insight into the publishing process and the role of the publisher. It can be an exhilarating but also an anxious time for an author. Above all, the publisher is also there as friend and confidant.

I wish you the very best of luck. Don't give up; dreams do come true, and remember, without you writers we publishers wouldn't be here.

WEEK 15

Writing for Stage

After twenty-something years of writing stories in book form I *sort* of know that the main thing is to keep the story going, move the plot on, not to go down alleyways, and not to introduce a cast of thousands. That's storytelling. But I can't begin to know what will work in a theater, so now you have a chance to learn firsthand.

Playwright Jim Culleton knows what works onstage—he has this extraordinary instinct about what will make people laugh or cry in an audience. I have no idea how he can look at lines written on a page and see which will work in a dark theater and which won't. Jim is very approachable, and has always been a great encouragement to new writers as well as working well with so-called established writers. Whenever he has taken my short stories and adapted them for the stage I thought they were hilarious, and laughed loudly and immoderately until the audience thought I was insane and very vain. But I was laughing not at my own words (which often looked very flat on the page) but at the way they were presented. So how do you go about writing for the stage?

1   *What do I write a play about?*   I know Jim Culleton believes that the best plays are on topics that we feel passionate about. People will write with conviction and ultimately much more success if it's on a subject dear to their hearts. There's no point in wondering what kind of themes might be more successful than others and saying, "Aha, that's what I'll write about." It just doesn't work. Remember all those plays in the last century that began with a maidservant dusting a telephone, and had people bouncing in through French windows asking who's for tennis? That all came about because a few successful comedies were set at posh house parties and then everyone thought they could do it.

2   *Do I need to know a playwriting technique?*   I think not. But I believe that if you go to a lot of theater yourself, and read plays, it will somehow sink in. You will learn, as I have half-learned, that people don't necessarily declaim; they don't make and finish a speech and then stand back to let another person make a similar speech. Rather they interrupt one another, leave sentences unfinished. You have no time in a play to write interior monologue, which is what I am heavily into. You know the kind of thing:

She looked at him, worried. Did he really love her, or was this life they had a total compromise? She would never really know, since he was good at hiding his feelings. Was it

*better not to challenge him, leave things as they were? Or
was this the worst way to go?*

I'm slightly sending myself up here, but you know what I
mean. In a play you can't give all this background information; you have to make it understood by giving the angst-
ridden woman some short line that will convey all of the
above.

3 *Do you need a large number of stage directions?*   Apparently
not. That's the director's or producer's job. And sometimes it's
the actor's job. They don't want us to write down every move
for them. If we get the dialogue right, it should all be there on
the page.

4 *Are there huge limitations on the time and place in which
we set a play?*   No, I believe it's meant to be much more
liberating than any other kind of writing. In a theater you can
change the whole time frame and have someone's childhood
or old age shown just by a change in lighting; or you can have
different events taking place in different settings. Again the
trick is to go to lots of plays and watch for the possibilities.

5 *Are we mad to think we might be playwrights?* Just as the
publishers are not sitting there laughing at our pathetic attempts to write but are actually dying to find something they
can publish and make money out of, so it is with theater folk.
They are aching for us to write something that will make
them hugely successful and the talk of the town. So all we
have to do is keep at it until we get it right.

Great good wishes and huge success.
Love from,

Maeve

- *The most successful playwrights are often those who began their writing career drawing from their own lives. They also understand the vital interaction between a live performance and the audience. Jim Culleton, the award-winning artistic director of Fishamble Theatre Company, examines how to give a play focus, and the unique collaboration between playwright, director, and actors.*

What Works Onstage

~

Jim Culleton

When I was asked to give advice to the Maeve Binchy Writers' Club about what works onstage, I remember thinking, "Well, if I knew the answer to that, every single play I direct would be a huge success." There are no rules for what will or won't work, but there are a few qualities I certainly look for in a play.

I have adapted Maeve's stories for the stage a few times, and it is always a very enjoyable process, as they capture so much of what works well onstage. They have very clearly defined characters, great dialogue, and—most important—Maeve has something heartfelt that she believes in passionately to say in each one. I think playwrights should have a strong vision of what they want to say and then the language and structure should express it in an engaging, exciting way. A director or dramaturge can help with the structure and character development, but the playwright should have the initial passion for communicating a unique view of the world.

The well-known advice that encourages "writing about what you know" has a lot of truth to it. Certainly, writing about what you know gives a personal and unique insight into human behavior and relationships and can give a strong sense of truthfulness to the writing. Some of the most successful first plays by new and emerging playwrights that I have directed have often explored situations with which the playwrights were familiar, mixed with their imaginative and creative insight, too.

When writing a play, I think it is best not to think of the play as words on a page, but rather of theater and its possibilities. Plays can be set anywhere—there are no boundaries. Playwrights should feel they can use the possibilities of the medium and visualize actors, set, lights, and sound as they are writing. As Maeve says, nothing beats going to the theater and seeing both what inspires you and what you would do differently as you develop your own theatrical voice.

In terms of how to structure a play, there are fascinating decisions for the playwright to make about the order of scenes and how information is revealed. Some interesting examples of this are the use of the flashback in plays like *Dancing at Lughnasa* by Brian Friel, *The Nun's Wood* by Pat Kinevane, and *Red Roses and Petrol* by Joseph O'Connor; the reversed chronology of scenes in *Betrayal* by Harold Pinter, a pub full of characters played by two actors in *Two* by Jim Cartwright; the way time and chronology are subverted in *Top Girls* by Caryl Churchill; the way information is revealed through interconnecting monologues in *The Pride of Parnell Street* by Sebastian Barry.

Once the playwright has something passionate to say, and works out how to say it, the next stage—hopefully—is producing the play. Theater is a live art form and a collaborative one. So it is not as solitary for the playwright as writing in other media can be. Moreover, in theater, directors, designers, and actors can help bring a new perspective to the play through their input. In working with playwrights on new plays, I find the most exciting writers are those who strike a balance between being clear and focused about their vision and yet open-minded about how the play evolves and grows as it moves toward being performed for an audience.

Often, in playwriting courses, new writers are encouraged to write a very short play (under ten minutes) that establishes a premise, explores the issue, and reaches a conclusion, as Samuel Beckett does in many of his short plays. Perhaps that is a good challenge for any new playwright wondering how to begin!

WEEK 16

⌒

Murder, Mystery, and Suspense

How I would love to be able to write a thriller, a story that would raise the hairs on the back of people's necks. But I'm bad at suspense. It's a personality thing, a bit like talking too much, wanting to tell everything a bit overeagerly—I'd give away the plot too soon.

I love reading thrillers. I *love* them, and usually read two or three a week. Recently I read John Grisham's *The Last Juror*, *Paranoia* by Joseph Finder, and a wonderful old-fashioned paperback called *Tragedy at Law* by Cyril Hare. I have even gone so far as to write down "Hints on Writing a Thriller," which I have in a notebook. Some of them have been there for twenty years, so I didn't exactly get on with it. In a fit of generosity I have decided to give you all my hints.

How do you create suspense?

Ed McBain wrote dozens of 87th Precinct and Matthew Hope novels. I interviewed him once and asked him if there was a rule. He said he had a trick, which was that you gave the reader more information than you gave the cops. Then the reader felt terrific at guessing what was happening before the detective worked it out. He advised against making the police into total fools, however. Evelyn Anthony, author of *The Tamarind Seed* and dozens of other novels, whom I also interviewed, said that she does suspense by preventing one set of people from knowing what's happening, so they are heading blithely into the jaws of some kind of danger that we readers know about, but the characters don't.

How do you do a surprise ending?

Agatha Christie (whom I did not interview, sadly) once wrote that she began each thriller with the chapter on the suspects' alibis, then she arranged that one of the alibis could be broken and that suspect would be the murderer. She worked out personality and motives later.

False alarms

When you are reading a good thriller you can approach heart failure over some perfectly simple false alarms. A creaking door could be a cat coming in, not an ax murderer; a flapping window could be a trapped crow, not a serial killer making an entrance. And then, just as we are calm again and breathing relatively easily, they pounce on us. Maybe that's something to set up.

Attention to detail

A lot of thriller writers like a fair amount of gory detail, and you need to get that right. Patricia Cornwell and Kathy Reichs have

audiences of millions for their pathology laboratory books, but you can be sure that every last detail is correct. Similarly, Len Deighton, Jack Higgins, and Frederick Forsyth will have the assassins' weaponry accurate—not a ball bearing out of place. If you choose a specialized area, like John le Carré chose the world of spies, you'd want to be sure to get it right. There are too many old pros out there reading books and just dying to write to the papers or the publishers to say you have it all wrong.

Bring in your own area of expertise

You don't have to throw out your own style just because you're writing a thriller. If you have a witty style, you could write a humorous thriller—or a woman's thriller or a travel thriller for that matter. There are endless permutations.

Those are my hints, but next you have something much better with advice from Julie Parsons. I used to know Julie way back when she was a nice, quiet girl, a producer for Ireland's public broadcaster, and there was no way of knowing she was destined to frighten us all out of our wits with her writing. What terrifies me so much about her books is that they are all set in so-called normal and familiar places, places like Blackrock and Dun Laoghaire. On the surface everything seems normal: that looks like an ordinary family; that looks like a reasonable couple. And then we discover that they are very far from the norm, indeed. So how does she do it? Does she have a master plan and tell herself exactly when she's going to pull the rug from under our feet?

Finally, remember that publishers and booksellers *love* the thriller as an art form. So good luck—you could well be the new Conan Doyle!

Love from,

Maeve

- *Thriller writers understand the bigger questions in life—including love, death, greed, and anger. They also know how to encapsulate these things into gripping plots and page-turning narrative. Julie Parsons, internationally published author and former radio and television producer, examines the crucial role of the imagination in thriller writing, and how to turn your ideas into plots.*

Writing Thrillers and Having Fun

Julie Parsons

When I talk to people about writing, they always ask why I write the kind of books I write, and where I get my ideas from. Neither question is easy to answer. I suppose one of the reasons for writing a particular kind of book is that you enjoy reading them. I have always loved thrillers—especially those that are called "psychological thrillers," the ones that are more concerned with motives and relationships, rather than the actual crime itself. My favorite authors are Patricia Highsmith, Ruth Rendell, and P. D. James, all of whom write the kind of books that I like both to read and to write. In fact, P. D. James puts it in an interesting way:

> E. M. Forster has written: "The king died and then the queen died is a story. The king died and the queen died of grief is a plot. The queen died and no one knew why until they discovered that it was of grief, is a mystery, a form capable of high development." To that I would add, the queen died and everyone thought it was of grief until they discovered the puncture wound in her throat. That is a murder mystery, and it too is capable of high development.

The most important thing to remember about writing anything is to use your imagination. No matter how much research you do, your imagination is what counts. John Mortimer, who wrote the famous Rumpole series, actually advises that you write the book and then do the research. Plots come from hard work. They won't develop by themselves. They need to be thought about, struggled over, worked on. I often use the "what if" method—I constantly ask myself, what if, what if, what if?

I also think that genre fiction, such as crime and mystery, is just as important and interesting as writing that is categorized as literary fiction. Thrillers deal with the really big subjects: death, violence, cruelty, good and evil. They are often all about important moral and ethical dilemmas. They invariably raise the question of nature versus nurture, heredity versus environment, and whether people are intrinsically good or bad.

Again, P. D. James expresses this very well. She says that all the motives for murder come under the letter *L*: love, lust, lucre, and loathing. She also says that the most dangerous emotion of all is not hatred, but love.

If you want to write a novel—in any genre—one thing is very important. You must be filled with desire. Writing novels is very hard work. It requires a huge amount of dedication. In order to carry the project through from start to finish you really have to *want* to do it. But it's important not to get too discouraged or put off by what seems to be the magnitude of the task ahead. E. L. Doctorow, author of *Ragtime*, puts it very well. He says that writing a novel is like driving in the country at night. All you see ahead is what is lit up by your headlights. But if you just keep following your lights you will eventually reach your destination.

Keep at it. Your hard work will be rewarded.

WEEK 17

The Importance of Language

I was at a funeral recently and heard a man speaking from the heart about his friend who had died. They had shared a love of the sea, and his words had a lot of maritime metaphors about tempests and storms and coming safely to harbor and back to shore. It was exceptionally moving, and thinking about it afterward I wondered why it had affected us all so much. I decided that, as well as its obvious sincerity, it was the careful choice of language and the way he had used words. He made sure that not only would we remember the content, the fact that we all missed

his friend who was a good man, but we would also remember the way it was said, the setting that the speech had been given in as well as the speech itself.

In my own writing, I have always been careless of how I choose words, believing that the important thing is to go on quickly while the idea is there, to tell the story, to get on with what happens, not to delay by rolling around a phrase until it pleases me, not inserting a nice melodious sentence just for the sake of it. I have often been afraid to pause and choose words that will appeal.

This is a definite if not deeply offensive flaw in my character that I hope I will not pass on to you. But if too much of it has stuck to you, then now is the time to shake it off. Gerald Dawe, a poet and scholar who really does love language, will help you release the vocabulary that you have inside you. Because he has read so much, and deals with words every day of his life, he will be able to encourage you and set your feet firmly and unself-consciously on the path to expressing yourself more fully. But first, here are a few thoughts of my own.

1   I wonder, do the Irish, or people living in Ireland, have a bigger word pool? Or is that madness? My own view is that it's a definite advantage to come from a culture that once spoke a language with no words for yes and no. You had to get around yes and no if you were speaking Irish, like saying it is or it isn't, or I will or I won't. It meant you had to say more and make longer sentences. Other people who came to Ireland both before and after J. M. Synge are taken with the slightly convoluted way we speak. They think that we can be fairly lyrical without even trying. So I regard that as a bit of a bonus.

2   Another advantage of being Irish is that we missed the Victorian bit that the British went through, of not talking

until you had something to say, or children being seen and not heard, or speaking only when you were spoken to. All of these notions are utterly alien to the Irish psyche. But is it good or bad for us? Perhaps those folk who take more time to think things through come up with better words. Perhaps we are, for all our much-admired fluency, just motormouths.

3 In one of Kurt Vonnegut's marvelous books—I think it's *The Sirens of Titan*—there is a tribe whose people use only words that they like the sound of. This was a great idea for a while, since they sounded so melodious, but the tribe died out because they had no way of communicating with one another. Words had no meaning, only good sounds. That always stuck with me as a possible danger.

Sometimes when you read very pretentious book reviews and articles there are words in them that *nobody* can understand. One I keep seeing and having to look up is "palimpsest." It means a manuscript in which old writing has been rubbed out to make room for new, or a monumental brass turned over for a new inscription. I know, I know, you're going to tell me that you use the word "palimpsest" every hour of your life. But to my mind, it's showing off and obscures language rather than enriches it.

Love from,

Maeve

- *A writer's job is essentially the skilled manipulation of words. The use of language can establish character, describe an atmosphere, drive a narrative forward, or impose a point of view. Gerald Dawe, Northern Irish writer and poet, discusses the use of language, and how the way in which you say something is as important as what you say.*

Less Is More

Gerald Dawe

For any prospective writer, the principal, most basic of issues is the use of language. I want to show you in as uncomplicated a way as possible that no matter what your objective is in writing—whether it's to please yourself, to communicate something to others, to make money, or to "be known"—the only really important issue is how you use language and how alert you are to different kinds of language.

First, let me issue a warning: I want you to think about how vulnerable language is to manipulation, distortion, and misuse. Have a look at George Orwell's great essay "Politics and the English Language." Then let me give you just one example of the weight of meaning transmitted by language. A few years ago the *Irish Times* published a letter in the aftermath of the IRA murder of Detective Garda Jerry McCabe, and it sums up perfectly the way words can be loaded with extra meaning. It's very short, so I reproduce it here in full:

February 19, 2004

Madam,

*The Sinn Féin TD Arthur Morgan writes compassionately
of the "prisoners convicted of involvement in the tragic
events that led to the death" of Garda McCabe. Is this
clumsy phrase a new euphemism for "convicted killers"?
Yours, etc.,*

Tony Allwright, Killiney, Co. Dublin

All writers, even unpublished, first-time writers, have to bear
in mind how language can be twisted and turned into propa-
ganda. By not saying how we see and hear things, of what we
know to be the case, we sidestep reality, and that is not good for
a writer—any writer.

Good writers are always good readers and good listeners.

No matter how naturally gifted you may be with, say, description, or plot, or characterization, the more you read, the better
your chances of learning more about what you want to say. All
writing is about learning—learning to do what you do *better*, trying out different forms, concentrating on the work at hand,
rather than the "impact" or reception it may or may not have.
This is equally true of fiction, nonfiction, and, of course, poetry.
Maybe in bringing a poet's experience to the subject, I can un-
derscore the need for all aspiring writers to focus on *how* they
were saying *what* they were writing.

Writing fiction is an extraordinary freedom; to sit down and
create characters, scenes, moods, feelings, ideas, beliefs, with
comic, tragicomic, lighthearted, serious, entertaining intention
must be one of the hallmarks of our human individuality. The
next step—to publish—is another day's work. I can't explore in
any detail that crucial stage, as others are doing that, except to
say that publication should be the final priority, not the first.

But to call upon the great cliché: at the end of the day, using language is very much like learning to listen, *really* listen, to other people, including, bizarrely, oneself. The last writer I want to recommend to you is the English poet W. H. Auden. This is a marvelous passage:

> *A genuine writer forgets a work as soon as he has completed it and starts to think of the next one; if he thinks about his past work at all, he is more likely to remember its faults rather than its virtues. . . . He needs approval of his work by others in order to be reassured that the vision of life he believes he has had is a true vision and not a self-delusion, but he can only be reassured by those whose judgment he respects.*

The Dyer's Hand, 1963; 1987

And so say all of us.

WEEK 18

∾

Writing for Children

There was once a theory that writing for children was somehow easier than writing for grown-ups. Not anymore there isn't. And there was once a belief that children's fiction was a quiet little backwater. J. K. Rowling has put an end to that theory. Today's children are well catered to, with thousands of books appearing every year and huge sections of bookshops devoted entirely to them. Children's authors have rightly gotten their place in the sun at last, and people have recognized that writing for future grown-ups is very important.

Even though I don't write specifically for children, I do know a fair bit about it because I'm married to a children's writer, Gordon Snell. The world of children's writing has a very different set of highs and lows from the so-called adult one. If you are giving a reading for children and they are bored, they don't just yawn or drop off to sleep as adults do, they get up and go away. Adults *always* ask you where you get your ideas, and are deeply disappointed with the reply, which is, "From all around you, from looking at things and people and listening to them." Children ask you more interesting things, like how much did you get paid and how many pencils did you use?

Children often read a favorite book over and over, getting

something new from it each time. That's a fearsome responsibility to have when you're writing a book for a young audience—the knowledge that they may well know your book by heart in a few weeks. You can't be lazy and let things go if someone's going to give it that much attention! Here are a few questions to think about if you want to write for children.

1   Do children need simpler language, or do they come to terms with words that they don't quite understand? Sometimes when we were young we'd come across an unfamiliar word and because of the sense of the story we'd get to know what the word meant. I remember years back there were often words used by A. A. Milne and Lewis Carroll that I didn't know, but I sort of *got* to know them. When writing for children, should we stretch them or adapt our vocabulary to suit theirs? I genuinely don't know.

2   Do children want us to use their particular slang? Would that make them identify better with the story? And if so, what kind of slang or colloquial speech should we use? It does change a lot, doesn't it? And they might be saying "deadly" one year and "gross" the next, but it could have changed utterly the following year. Is it wiser not to explore the slang minefield at all?

3   Is there still a huge difference between what boys and what girls read? Nowadays is there a blurring of the lines?

4   How do you avoid patronizing children? Roald Dahl certainly knew how, as does Judy Blume and the whole galaxy of

successful and popular children's writers these days. I think it's hard if you're a teacher to begin with. You start trying to improve them, trying sneakily to teach them something. They can smell a teacher a mile off. They'd have me sussed in two minutes.

5   These days children all love electronic games, and texting one another, and watching television programs during which you can phone in, so how can we hope to engage them in something that's not interactive? Or is it the same as in the adult world—like the Death of the Book that everyone feared so much and which just hasn't happened?

As with all writing, the best advice I can give is to read other authors you admire in the same field, and see how they deal with these questions.

Only two more letters from me—my genuine congratulations that you've stuck with it. You *deserve* to be successful because you have taken on board the notion that it's all about keeping your bottom on that chair and refusing to give up.

Love from,

Maeve

WEEK 19

◦

Writing Comedy

Oh, to be able to make people laugh at will! Wouldn't it be wonderful? To see a lot of glum faces and turn them magically into happy ones! No wonder great comedians and gag writers are paid a fortune. No wonder Hollywood gets so excited about a zany or wacky comedy with someone like Steve Martin, Woody Allen, Eddie Murphy, or Ben Stiller. Is it any surprise that publishers yearn to find the book they can call the comic novel of the year? But how to do it? That is really the question.

There really *is* such a thing as the art of writing comedy. I think the worst job in the world, worse even than being a dentist or a miner, must be to be a stand-up comic. Imagine standing up and telling what you thought were jokes and people not laughing! An audience of them not laughing. It makes me feel weak and as if I were going to vomit at the very thought. Suppose you think something is funny and nobody else does? Does that make you mad, or make them mad?

I remember telling a story once that I thought was hilarious. I still feel the sweat on the back of my neck at the memory of it. Everyone stared at me politely, waiting for the punch line—after I had delivered it, long, long after. I wanted the world to end. I remember thinking, "It has to end *sometime*; why not now?" But it didn't, and I had to get on with living, and I swore I would never try anything funny again. But we swear things and we forget them. And so when I recovered I tried again, and sometimes I got a laugh, and it was so heady and so wonderful that it was all worth it!

But writing comedy is different. We aren't there to see and hear whether anyone is laughing or not, and so it's equally diffi-cult for a publisher to know whether or not something is going to entertain the readers. All right, we would all love to have people splitting their sides at what we write, and if there were any easy way then surely someone would have discovered it. Why was *Seinfeld* such a scream for so many people? And *Friends* and *The Office* and *The Simpsons* and *Cheers*? Was it the characters themselves? Or the plot situations? If we knew, we could do it, too. But we don't know, so we have to try to find out—without copying other writers—what on earth makes people laugh.

1   Sometimes I think they'll laugh if we make ourselves look foolish, vulnerable, and a bit silly. One of my most successful articles in the *Irish Times* was about not knowing whether to make the bed if you stayed in a hotel. It was utterly true. I had never stayed in a hotel until I was twenty-two. I sort of straightened the bed and folded back the covers, nothing that would destroy me as a hotel visitor. To my amazement, half the country seemed to have had the same dilemma, and they were delighted with me and told me I was a wonderfully humorous person, whereas in fact I had been telling the unvarnished truth in the hope that it would make people less self-conscious rather than amuse them.

2   Sometimes people laugh if you can create a truly funny character, like a clown figure, somebody you are meant to laugh at. But this is very hard to do. If you go over the top and make that person into a caricature then it's not really funny anymore; it's only a stereotype. You keep thinking that if that person were played by Bette Midler or Barbra Streisand she

would be a scream. But she's not being played by them; she's just by herself on the pages of your manuscript. You have to make her so appealing that readers like her as she is without any first-rate comediennes delivering her lines. I've tried saying  lines aloud to see if they're funny. Half the time it doesn't work—maybe more than half the time—but it's worth giving it a go.

3 As a journalist, over the years I have interviewed lots of funny people for the newspaper. They all said, every single one of them, that they had no idea whether something was funny or not until they tried it out.

All writing takes courage. Maybe comic writing just takes more courage than the other sort.

Love from,

Maeve

- *Comedy has been used for centuries as a way to entertain, to satirize, and as a defense against tragedy. One of the greatest skills a writer can have is an ability to recognize comedy when he or she sees it. Comic author Ferdia Mac Anna offers some tips for the budding comic writer.*

Writing Comedy

Ferdia Mac Anna

1 Write about what you know—and that includes your family (especially your family).

2 Ignore the facts.

3 Use your imagination, and don't let anyone or anything put you off.

4 Break your routine. Whenever you feel yourself settling into a groove, go for a walk or phone someone you hate or attend the wedding of a complete stranger.

5 Enjoy what you write. Because if you do, there's a really good chance that the reader will, too.

6 Always remember George Bernard Shaw's famous remark about comedy: "Always tell the truth—it's the funniest joke of all."

Enjoy!

WEEK 20

◡

Good Luck

Well, now, does it seem like a lifetime since we began? Or did it go by far too quickly, before you came to grips with it all properly? In any event—congratulations! Well-done for sticking with it. The very fact that you stayed means that you have a real commitment to being a writer. It's more than just a pious wish now. You've invested the time and effort and therefore proved that you do take it seriously.

I hope that in the marvelous selection of contributors you found not only inspiration but consolation. It's surely helpful to know that it's not easy for *anyone*, and that you aren't the only one who has been insulted by rejection. It's part of the training process. I am sure you learned from everyone, whichever side of the editorial process they are on, that they know rejection is worse than failing any exam because it's so personal. And yet it's our testing ground. There is no structure in which we pass or fail; we just have to keep hoping and keep sending stuff out.

What will separate the winners from the losers is that ability to pick ourselves up and refuse to take the rejection personally. The courage to say, "Well, that person may or may not be right, but I'm not going to stop." The very fact that someone has dared to send you back the beloved manuscript you slaved over and told you, though not in so many words, that it was useless is obviously a blow, but if this book has taught you that it happens to everyone, then it has probably given you hope rather than despair. I wish that hope stays with you always. It is what will eventually draw out of you the book, the stories, the writing that are in there waiting to be released.

None of us ever stops learning. For my last novel I got seven pages of closely typed corrections or suggested rewrites from the publisher. Now, this is after many books, so it goes on and on! I read them humbly and changed everything that I was asked to. It doesn't get any easier to do rewrites, but then we don't necessarily get any better. I *still* forget to give personal descriptions of people; I know what they look like, so I assume everyone else does. I *still* forget that you have to get people from one place to another, even a sentence saying that they went to the harbor, or they went back to her flat. I always think the reader knows automatically where the scene is taking place.

I promised to write twelve short stories this year. I have six of them written, two of them published, and one commissioned for the radio. And each week I wrote a letter to you, which I actually enjoyed very much. It made me think seriously about the job I

do and how it's done. For the last twenty-five years, I suppose I've been a bit on autopilot and I just get on with it. It was a challenge to try to think for you and for myself what technique is involved in writing a short story; what your relationship with an agent should be like; how to set up a thriller. I had to think hard about what works onstage.

The idea of this book is to take the terror out of writing, to empower ourselves with the belief that we are as good as anyone else, with as much to say as the next person. The only thing that stands in our way is *not* saying it. I hope you think it was all worth it and that you will never be among those who say that you could have written if only you had had the chance. The chance was offered to you, and you took it up bravely and enthusiastically. From now on, when we see one another's books in the shops we will take a vow to move them to the front of the store.

Solidarity is everything.

Love and well-done,

Maeve

CONTRIBUTORS' BIOGRAPHIES

Maeve Binchy was born in County Dublin and was educated at the Holy Child convent in Killiney and at University College, Dublin. After a spell as a teacher in various girls' schools, she joined the *Irish Times*, for which she still writes occasional columns. Her first novel, *Light a Penny Candle*, was published in 1982, and since then she has written more than a dozen novels and short story collections, each one of them bestsellers, including her recent novel, *Heart and Soul*. Several have been adapted for cinema and television, most notably *Circle of Friends* and *Tara Road*. Maeve Binchy was awarded the Lifetime Achievement Award at the British Book Awards in 1999. She is married to the writer and broadcaster Gordon Snell.

Ivy Bannister's stories and plays have been published and performed widely in Ireland, England, America, and Germany. For her stories, she has won the Francis MacManus award, the Hennessy award and various other fiction prizes. Around thirty stories have been broadcast by RTE and the BBC, and her story "What Big Teeth" was recently made into a short film in the United States. A collection of her stories, *Magician*, has been published in Ireland.

Carole Baron is an editor at Knopf. Formerly president of G. P. Putnam's Sons and Dutton, as well as president and publisher of Dell/Delacorte, she has worked with many bestselling authors, including Jean M. Auel, Maeve Binchy, Judy Blume, Tracy Chevalier, Harlan Coben, John Grisham, Thomas Harris, Amy Tan, and Danielle Steel.

Chris Bohjalian is the author of eleven novels, including the *New York Times* bestsellers *Skeletons at the Feast, The Double Bind, Before You Know Kindness, The Law of Similars,* and *Midwives.* His next book is titled *Remind Me Who I Am.*

Paula Campbell is a publisher with Poolbeg, one of Ireland's leading book publishers. Poolbeg publishes bestselling novels in the fiction, children's, romantic fiction, nonfiction, and literary fiction genres.

Norah Casey is Chief Executive of Harmonia. A Dublin-based company, it is the largest consumer and contract publishing house in Ireland, publishing a range of consumer titles, including *Irish Tatler, Woman's Way, U, Food & Wine, Auto Ireland, Auto Woman, Your New Baby,* and many contract publications, including *CARA* for Aer Lingus.

Jim Culleton is Artistic Director of Fishamble: The New Play Company and is responsible for the Dublin company's distinctive and riveting vision. Fishamble has presented multi-award-winning new work in Dublin, and to audiences in the United Kingdom, throughout Ireland, the United States, France, Germany, and the Czech Republic.

Gerald Dawe is the author of seven collections of poetry, including *Sheltering Places, The Morning Train, Lake Geneva,* and *Points West.* His second collection, *The Lundys Letter,* was awarded the Macaulay Fellowship in Literature. Other awards include an Arts Council Bursary for Poetry, the Hawthornden International Writers' Fellowship, and the Ledig-Rowholt International Writers' Award. In 2007 he published a volume of collected criticism, *The Proper Word*, and a memoir, *My Mother-City*. He lectures in English at the University of Dublin, Trinity College, where he is director of the Oscar Wilde Centre for Irish Writing and director of the graduate creative writing program.

Marian Keyes is the internationally bestselling author of nine novels, including *Watermelon, Rachel's Holiday, The Last Chance Saloon, Sushi for Beginners, Anybody Out There?*, and *This Charming Man*. Her books have touched readers around the world, and they are published in thirty-five different languages. Over twelve million copies of her books have been sold worldwide.

Ferdia Mac Anna is a well-known published author. His novels are *The Last of the High Kings, The Ship Inspector*, and *Cartoon City*. The film of *The Last of the High Kings* was released in 1996. He has edited *The Penguin Book of Comic Irish Writing*, and has published two memoirs, *Bald Head, A Cancer Story* and *The Last of the Bald Heads*.

Julie Parsons is an internationally published author. Her novels are *Mary, Mary, The Courtship Gift, Eager to Please, The Guilty Heart, The Smoking Room, The Hourglass*, and *I Saw You*. A former producer with RTE radio and television, she lives in Dublin.

AFTERWORD

A Final Word of Thanks from the National College of Ireland

We are hugely appreciative of the time, effort, and expertise devoted by the contributors to this book.

This breakthrough project was envisaged by my predecessor, Professor Joyce O'Connor, through the friendship established with Maeve Binchy. For some time now Maeve Binchy has been a staunch supporter of the National College of Ireland. She has been hugely generous with her personal time and resources, based on a fundamental commitment to supporting what we are trying to do. Those who know Maeve will also acknowledge her gift as an inspiring coach (and she's not bad fun either!).

National College of Ireland is a not-for-profit, third-level educational institution that was founded by the Jesuit Order in 1951. It was established as the "workers' college," with the explicit purpose of training employees and managers, side by side, in an effort to promote mutual understanding and reduce the high levels of conflict that were endemic at that time. As the world of work changed, the college expanded from its early industrial-relations base. It is a challenging task to constantly "balance the books," and it would not be possible without the enormous generosity of our supporters.

Incredibly, everyone involved waived their entire fee in order to bring this book to life. I would like to thank each of the key contributors both to the course and to this book for their expertise and time given so selflessly (Ivy Bannister, Pat Boran, Paula Campbell, Norah Casey, Marita Conlon-McKenna, Jim Culleton, Gerald Dawe, Marian Keyes, Ferdia Mac Anna, Mary Morrisy, Julie Parsons, Deirdre Purcell, Peter Sheridan, Jonathan Williams, Peter Woods, and Willie Rocke. We are also delighted that for the American edition Carole Baron and Chris Bohjalian have been added to the roster). Each of the above have their fingerprints on this innovative project. Hopefully we've managed to capture the essence of their input with some degree of rigor. Sarah Eustace (former assistant to Joyce O'Connor) was the project manager at the college. Once the journal was pulled into manuscript form all the "technical stuff" (structural editing, copy editing, negotiating, and the royalty fees) was handled with ease and some style by Maeve's longtime agent, Christine Green. The complex publication process was simplified under the expert guidance of Juliet Ewers. And the American edition owes a debt of thanks to Jennifer Jackson, senior editor at Vintage and Anchor Books, and Carole Baron.

To each of the above, a sincere thank you.

Dr. Paul Mooney
President, National College of Ireland

SUGGESTED FURTHER READING

The Cambridge Introduction to Creative Writing by David Morley, Cambridge University Press, 2007.

The Complete Idiot's Guide to Writing a Novel by Tom Monteleone, Alpha Books, 2004.

The Creative Writing Handbook by John Singleton, Mary Luckhurst (eds), Palgrave Macmillan, 1999.

Creative Writing: A Practical Guide by Julia Casterton, Palgrave Macmillan, 2005.

From Pitch to Publication by Carole Blake, Pan Books, 1999.

How to Be a Brilliant Writer by Jenny Alexander, A&C Black, 2005.

How to Write Damn Good Fiction: Advanced Techniques for Dramatic Storytelling by James N. Frey, Pan Books, 2002.

How to Write a Novel by John Braine, Methuen, 1974.

On Writing by Stephen King, New English Library, 2001.

Reading Like a Writer: A Guide for People Who Love Books and for Those Who Want to Write Them by Francine Prose, Harper Perennial, 2007.

The Road to Somewhere: A Creative Writing Companion by Robert Graham, Helen Newall, Heather Leach, Julie Armstrong, and John Singleton, Palgrave Macmillan, 2004.

The Routledge Creative Writing Coursebook by Paul Mills, Routledge, 2005.

Talking About Detective Fiction by P. D. James, Alfred A. Knopf, 2009.

Teach Yourself Creative Writing by Dianne Doubtfire and Ian Burton, Teach Yourself Books, 2003.

This Year You Write Your Novel by Walter Mosley, Little, Brown, 2007.

The Writing Experiment: Strategies for Innovative Creative Writing by Hazel Smith, Allen & Unwin, 2005.

Writing Fiction: A Guide to Narrative Craft by Janet Burroway and Elizabeth Stuckey-French, Longman, 2006.

Writing Fiction: Creative and Critical Approaches by Amanda Boulter, Palgrave Macmillan, 2007.

Writing Logically, Thinking Critically by Sheila Cooper and Rosemary Patton, Longman, 2006.

Writing a Novel by Nigel Watts, Teach Yourself Books, 2006.

A SELECTION OF WRITING
COMPETITIONS, AWARDS, ETC.

Long Fiction and Novels

The AWP Grace Paley Prize in Short Fiction and the Novel
http://www.awpwriter.org/contests/series.htm
An annual competition for the publication of book-length works,
open to all authors writing in English regardless of nationality or
residence. Deadline: February.

Flannery O'Connor Award for Short Fiction
http://www.ugapress.uga.edu/
Run by the University of Georgia Press. Authors of winning
manuscripts receive a cash award and their collections are
subsequently published by the press under a standard book contract.
Deadline: May.

Juniper Prize in Fiction
http://www.umass.edu/umpress/juniper_fiction.html
The winning author receives a cash award, a contract with standard
royalties, and an invitation to read at the University of
Massachusetts's Visiting Writers Series. Deadline: September.

The *Writer's Digest* International Self-Published Book Award
http://www.writersdigest.com/selfpublished
The only competition exclusively for self-published books. Deadline:
May.

Short Fiction

American Short Fiction Short Story Contest
http://www.americanshortfiction.org
Judged by the editorial staff of *American Short Fiction,* this award
highlights great work in stories of a thousand words or less.
Deadline: May.

Boulevard Short Fiction Contest for Emerging Writers
http://www.richardburgin.net/1boulevardsfcontest.htm
Awarded to writers who have not yet published a book of
fiction, poetry, or creative nonfiction. The winning author
receives a cash award and publication in *Boulevard.* Deadline:
December 31.

Glimmer Train Open Fiction Contest
http://glimmertrain.stores.yahoo.net/fictionopen.html
Quarterly contest open to all writers and all themes.

Katharine Anne Porter Prize in Short Fiction
http://web3.unt.edu/untpress/potential_authors.cfm
Established by the University of North Texas Press, this annual
award includes a cash award and publication by UNT Press.
Deadline: June.

The Mary McCarthy Prize in Short Fiction
http://www.sarabandebooks.org/contest/mary_mccarthy_prize.html
The Mary McCarthy Prize in Short Fiction includes a cash award
and publication of the winning short story collection, novella, or
novel under standard royalty contract. Run by Sarabande Books.
Deadline: February.

The *Narrative* Prize
http://www.narrativemagazine.com/node/421
The Narrative Prize is awarded annually for the best short story,
novel excerpt, poem, or work of literary nonfiction published by a
new or emerging writer. Deadline: June 15.

The Robert Olen Butler Short Fiction Prize
http://delsolpress.org/dsp-fictionprizewinners.htm
Established by Del Sol, this prize is awarded for the best short story, either published (in a periodical) or unpublished. The winner receives a cash honorarium and publication in Del Sol's annual anthology. Deadline: December.

The *Writer's Digest* Short Short Story Competition
http://www.writersdigest.com/short
An annual award with many winners. Deadline: December.

Playwriting

The *Arts & Letters* Prize in Drama
http://al.gcsu.edu/prizes.htm
An award for one-act plays. Winner receives a cash award, production, and publication in the *Arts & Letters* journal. Deadline: April.

Aurand Harris Memorial Playwriting Award
http://www.netconline.org
For unpublished work intended for young audiences and not produced professionally, this annual award comes with a cash prize. Deadline: May.

Fremont Centre Theatre New Playwright Contest
http://www.fremontcentretheatre.com
A contest for full-length plays, one-acts, and plays for young audiences. The winner receives a cash award and a staged reading. Special consideration for plays based on historical events, persons, or moments; plays about the African-American experience, modern or historical; and comedies. Deadline: April.

The Pen Is a Mighty Sword New Play Competition
http://www.virtualtheatreproject.com
A competition for full-length plays with several winners. Deadline: February.

Reva Shiner Full-Length Play Contest
http://www.newplays.org
A contest for full-length plays and musicals, with a special interest in
innovative work and small-scale musicals. Deadline: October.

Magazines

African American Review
http://aar.slu.edu./

AGNI
http://www.bu.edu/agni/

American Profile
http://www.americanprofile.com/

Asimov's Science Fiction
http://www.asimovs.com/

Brick
http://www.brickmag.com./

Christian Science Monitor
http://www.csmonitor.com/

Cincinnati Review
http://www.cincinnatireview.com/

Colorado Review
http://coloradoreview.colostate.edu/

Crazyhorse
http://crazyhorse.cofc.edu/

Ellery Queen Mystery Magazine
http://www.themysteryplace.com/eqmm/

Fantasy & Science Fiction
http://www.sfsite.com/fsf/

Girls' Life
http://www.girlslife.com/

Indiana Review
http://indianareview.org/

Inkwell
http://www.inkwelljournal.org/

Kenyon Review
http://www.kenyonreview.org/

Literary Bohemian
http://www.literarybohemian.com/

Mississippi Review
http://www.mississippireview.com/

Narrative
http://narrativemagazine.com/

One Story
http://one-story.com/

Parents.com
American Baby, Parents, Family Circle
http://www.parents.com/

The Paris Review
http://www.theparisreview.org/

Ploughshares
http://www.pshares.org/

Reader's Digest
http://www.rd.com

The Southern Review
http://www.lsu.edu/thesouthernreview/

Tin House
http://www.tinhouse.com/

TriQuarterly
http://www.triquarterlyto-day.blogspot.com/

Water-Stone Review
http://www.waterstonereview.com/

WOW! Women on Writing
http://wow-womenonwriting.com/

Zahir
http://www.zahirtales.com/

Zoetrope: All-Story
http://www.all-story.com/index.cgi

Helpful Web Sites

Absolute Write
http://www.absolutewrite.com

Blogger
http://www.blogger.com

Critique Circle Online Writing Workshop
http://www.critiquecircle.com

Freelance Writing Jobs
http://www.freelancewritingjobs.com

LitMatch
http://www.litmatch.net

MediaBistro
http://www.mediabistro.com

Practicing Writer
http://www.practicing-writer.com/

The Purdue University Online Writing Lab
http://owl.english.purdue.edu/

TypePad
http://www.typepad.com

WordPress
http://www.wordpress.org

Writer Beware
http://www.sfwa.org/for-authors/writers-beware/

WritersMarket.com
http://www.writersmarket.com

Stories and Columns
by Maeve Binchy

Seven Stories

I suppose, like everything, it's up to you what you bring to and take from a writers' group.
—Maeve Binchy

The Writing Class

The woman on the radio made it all sound so easy. It was a matter of having a beginning, a middle, and an end, having some sort of a plot, and listening carefully to the way people talked. All over the country they listened to her, and people's hearts soared.

A class that would teach you to be a writer, it was *exactly* what so many people were looking for. Women in their kitchens preparing supper paused to write down the telephone number; students meant to be doing last-minute revisions scribbled it down on their ring binders. Men stuck in jobs that they hated wrote it down and dreamed of the day they would have a book party and invite only those they had liked in the office. Motorists pulled onto the side of the road to write down the number.

It seemed like money for old rope.

Nancy was none of the above. Nancy was packing her things to leave Ed's apartment, where she had lived for three years. It was over, Ed had told her, and there was no point in trying to pretend otherwise. It was time for everyone to move on. And they should do it sooner rather than later.

Ed wasn't moving on. He was moving a new person in. He asked Nancy to be gone by Saturday. He would leave her a couple of days to sort it out on her own. New beginnings for everyone, he had said cheerfully. He would change the locks on the door Saturday morning. Better that way.

Nancy was going through the bookshelves taking her books, which was most of them. She looked through the CDs: most were his, but she would leave them all. It looked like a big, generous gesture on her part. In fact she would never want to hear the music they had played together. Never again.

She thought about the bedspread. It had been very expensive but it had been a birthday present from her to Ed. She wouldn't take that. The picture they had bought in a gallery in Cornwall. They had each paid half. She wouldn't want it on a wall in her new life; it would remind her too much of those magical days in little Cornish harbors when the world was full of hope and sunshine and promise. The saucepans? His, really. Towels? She didn't want them. Just her clothes, and the books and a few ornaments. Not much to show for three years. Not much to take to her new quarters.

She had rented a big bed-sitter with a tiny kitchen and an even smaller bathroom attached. She was telling nobody how it had ended, how cold and detached Ed had been, how he would dare to change the locks as if she would ever come back here again. She could not humiliate herself by admitting that she had lived three years with such a man.

None of her friends liked him; nobody at work knew about him. Nancy worked in a florist's shop. The woman who ran it was very reserved, and she discouraged any chat about people's private lives. In many ways it had been a relief. No need to explain that Ed had gone away without her yet again, or that there was no sign of a ring or a commitment of any kind.

Nancy looked at the radio. His, if you were being honest. But then he had taken her old radio and traded it in for a better one. So now she had no radio. She wondered if she would take it. Maybe it would be petty. Better leave with an aura of generosity. Even though Ed had shown very little sign of it. It had good tone, that radio. Nancy switched it on for a last time and heard the woman talking about the writing class.

That's what she would do. She would write a bestseller. Ed would see her books in the windows of the bookstores; he would see big feature articles about her in newspapers and magazines; he would turn on the television and see her on chat shows. He would learn of the huge advances she would get for each novel and what a fortune she was earning.

Ed loved money. He would be very regretful that he had sent her out of his life. And changed the locks. Very. Let him have the radio. She had written down the number she needed on the back of a picture of her that he still had in the bedroom. She had left the frame so that he could put the next girl in it. Nancy wondered, would she last three years?

Then she called a taxi, locked the door for the last time, and put the soon-to-be-useless keys back through the letter box.

Jane ran a bed-and-breakfast business. It was tiring and it was hard work, but it was a living, and she actually enjoyed meeting the people who came in and out. At the moment she was full, all four rooms occupied. Two with eager Scandinavians, couples who had, it seemed, already walked the length and breadth of the city and were setting out to walk still farther. One bedroom was taken by a wordless man who came up from the country for four nights every week, and no secret police of any country could prize from him what his business was.

The fourth room was for Lilly and her six-month-old baby, Sophie. Jane hadn't really wanted to take welfare people and have the house full of screaming children. But Lilly was so young and the baby so quiet that she had no excuse. When the other guests had finished breakfast, Lilly helped with the washing-up and making the beds. In return, Jane gave her full use of the washing machine, dryer, and the kitchen. It worked well as long as nobody suspected. Jane got paid by the authorities, poor Lilly and Sophie, the baby, had something near a home, and nobody lost out.

Jane had never trained for any career. She had always looked after her own mother, who had been poorly for as long as anyone remembered. And then when Jane was forty, Mother died and there she was with no real way of earning a living. Her brothers had shrugged; Jane had lived in Mother's house for all those years when they had to go out and buy places of their own. It had all turned out very well when you came to think of it. Yes, very well indeed. An empty house and no qualifications.

So she started the bed-and-breakfast. She went to computer classes and learned how to get visitors on the Internet. She considered borrowing from the bank and putting on three more rooms at the back, but eight people was manageable for breakfast. And she had grown fond of Lilly and Sophie. Building work would be too disruptive for a baby.

Jane didn't have extravagant tastes; she didn't really need more money. All she needed was the sharpness of mind to make sure that her clients weren't the sort who would empty the house of her simple belongings. And really, the B and B business wasn't that bad. You were finished by eleven in the morning, with the house clean and the shopping done for tomorrow's breakfast.

Jane took in ironing in the afternoons. Her own little bed-sitting room had two clothes racks in it, and she had gotten to enjoy the smell of freshly ironed shirts. Sometimes she offered a guest the luxury of ironing something for them, and they nearly fainted with delight. So she was at her ironing board when she heard the item on the radio. It doesn't matter what kind of a life you lead, the woman appeared to be saying, if you could tell it like a story, it would work.

Jane paused, iron in hand. *That's* what she would do this autumn. Join a writing class.

Vincent and his son, Gerry, listened to the item in the car as they drove home from the graveyard. It was the first anniversary of

Sheila's death. They had gone to put flowers on her grave. They had hoped it might make them feel better, but it had made them feel worse.

"You were a great wife," Vincent had said to the small Celtic cross over the grave.

"You were a great mam," Gerry mumbled, as if they were lines from a school play. He had been in the school dramatic society before, but somehow since Mam's death he hadn't the heart for it.

He had nothing to say to his father and his father had no words for him. They were driving back to the house that seemed to have no soul in it these days.

Vincent turned on the car radio. "We might as well be listening as not," he said.

"Sure, Da."

It was some writer telling them about a class that taught you how to write a book. They both listened because it was easier than trying to talk when there was nothing to say. Eventually the woman was replaced by someone else who was talking about keeping llamas in your garden. Apparently you could have four llamas per acre. Vincent and Gerry managed a watery smile over that as an idea.

Then Vincent said, "You know, your mother always said I should write a book about my adventures on the road."

"Did she now, Da?" Gerry wondered what possible adventures his quiet father could have had as a traveling salesman driving a van all over the country.

"She said it was a story of the old times, before marketing came in and changed everything," he said.

"Well, maybe you should join up at the class then." Gerry wanted to get his father out of the house for some sort of thing. This might be as good as any.

"I'd be afraid to go on my own, I don't have any confidence going to social things anymore. Would you come with me, son? Maybe they could get a book out of you, too?"

His father was pleading. He had never seen this before. Gerry heard himself saying that he'd love to go.

"A pity we didn't write down the phone number," said Vincent, who seemed very pleased by this decision.

"I wrote it down; I've got it here," Gerry said, and the car was a lighter place once the plan had been agreed.

In the radio studio they were packing up.

"The llama piece was nice," the series producer said approvingly.

"I thought your woman who was doing the writing class was good," said the presenter, Clare.

"Oh, God, no, another one of these 'everyone's got a book in them' gurus." The series producer had seen it all, done it all, and was impressed by nothing.

"Maybe we all have," the presenter said defensively.

"Oh, please, Lord, then let's hope that everyone keeps the book well buried inside them, rather than releasing it."

The series producer was busy putting on lip gloss. She was going to have cocktails with some very smart people who were thinking of putting money into an independent production company. This just might be the big crossroads in her life. She had little time to make idle chat with Clare, a girl who was fast on her way to nowhere. She hadn't noticed that Clare had written down the phone number of the writing class and had every intention of joining.

On the first night of the writing class they heard that they didn't have to pay their fees until the first lecture was over. This would give them a chance to know whether or not the course was right for them. There were questions they would want to ask. Nobody should join unless absolutely certain that this was the right course. At the end, almost everyone signed up.

They were put into groups of five. The hope was that they

would help and encourage one another if anyone was failing to write the ten pages a week that they would be expected to produce.

The first week would be an easy assignment: they were to go around bookshops and libraries and see what kind of book they might possibly write. They were to list the publishers they might approach; then they were to write a letter to an imaginary friend telling the story.

They were urged to introduce themselves to their group. Clare the radio presenter met Nancy, a florist; Jane, who ran a small B and B; Vincent and his son, Gerry. Vincent was a salesman, his son about to go to university. They all had coffee and biscuits and reassured one another that they weren't completely mad to be doing this.

Next week they would all meet again and read one another the letter to the imaginary friend; then they would have a lecture from a publisher listing the most common mistakes people make when submitting work.

"I suppose we should think of it like Weight Watchers or Alcoholics Anonymous," said Jane.

Vincent nodded thoughtfully. "Great people, those AA folk," he said. "My wife was a member and they would go out in the middle of the night to help one another."

Gerry's head shot up in alarm. His father rarely mentioned his dead wife, and to Gerry's certain knowledge had never told anyone of her alcoholism.

Nancy rescued the moment. "Right—if we are going to be open all hours then we should give everyone our mobile phone numbers," she said in a businesslike way.

They went home into the dark.

Nancy went past Ed's flat to see if the light was on in the bedroom. If it was dark, that meant they were in bed making love. If the light was on, then it meant that they were so confident with each other they were making love with the lights on.

Jane went back to the house where she had lived so long with her mother, a house with a B and B sign swinging in the night air now. She hoped that Lilly was up so they could have tea and maybe toast and honey. But the house was silent. The Scandinavians were absolutely exhausted from pacing the city. The wordless man from the country was asleep dreaming of the Lord knew what. From Lilly's room, Jane heard muffled tears. It was one of those nights when Lilly's broken heart was hurting worse than usual, and she was wondering why the boy had run away from her and baby Sophie.

Clare the radio presenter went home to her parents' house where she lived fairly peaceably with her mother. Except for the times when her mother was urging her to get married. Tonight turned out to be one of those nights.

"I suppose it was all women at the class," she said glumly.

"There were some men there, but you're right, it was mainly female."

"Not much hope of meeting anyone there, then."

"No, Mother, but then that's not what I went there for; I'm going to learn how to write a book."

"Huh," said Clare's mother.

"Leave the girl alone," said Clare's father. "She has plenty of time to meet someone."

"And when I do want to meet someone I'll go online or answer a lonely-hearts ad, so don't panic, Mum." Clare wished they had asked her about the evening. But she was a grown-up woman of twenty-four now, not a child anymore. It was silly wishing for impossible things.

Vincent and Gerry went into their house, where so many promises had been made and broken about alcohol. Where there had always been secrecy, and new hopes that had not materialized. Vincent took out a couple of cans of beer. Gerry's eyes opened wide. Because of Mam there had never been any form of alcohol in this house.

"We have to move on, Gerry, lad," his father said. "If we're going to write ten pages a week, then by God we need something to get us started."

The next Tuesday they all turned up in good time and settled around the little table in the hall. They all had their ten pages ready.

Nancy read her story-letter. It was about a good woman who was involved with a monstrously selfish man. She then made a great deal of money, and he was sorry that he had let her go and begged her to come back. But she wouldn't. Then he fell on hard times so she relented, returned good for evil, and went back to him.

The other four looked at her blankly.

"It's not very likely, is it?" Jane asked. "I mean, I know nothing really about anything except serving eight cooked breakfasts a morning, but why would this woman go back to him if he was so awful? Wouldn't she be far better off on her own?"

Clare said she thought if we were meant to think the heroine was barking mad and heading for the funny farm we should be told more. It couldn't be the twenty-first century. Women didn't do that kind of martyr thing anymore.

Vincent said that it hadn't been made clear in the outline whether the woman and the monstrous man had a really wonderful thing going between them once and it had drifted away because of some problem.

Gerry said he thought it would be a better story if the woman were to kill the monstrous man. Maybe by electrocuting him in the bath. It could be written in such a way that we would be a bit sorry for the woman, and hope she got only a short time in the mental home.

Nancy was very disappointed with this reaction, but she nailed a smile on her face. And they went on to hear Clare's story.

Clare had written about a woman who had a job at the reception desk of a big insurance company. A horrible woman senior executive in the company was constantly putting her down, so life wasn't very cheerful. At home things weren't much better. She had parents who were very much on her case for still being single. They made her feel a failure. What she really wanted was a chance to live in a big house with lots of other young people, like in the television sitcoms. And then one day there was an advertisement for flatmates and she found exactly what she was looking for.

Jane always tried to say something nice, but she wondered if this was a touch unrealistic. If this receptionist was so good, why didn't she just get on with things at work? And if she hated being at home, why didn't she just move out? She must have some friends to move in with rather than finding the advertisement. . . .

Nancy didn't want Clare to think that she was reacting badly just because her own story had been shot down in flames. But she did say gently that the heroine lacked any sense of purpose, and if we were meant to identify with her she'd have to do something more than complain.

Vincent said that there was no mention at all of how the heroine related to her parents. Did she like them or just resent them? After all, they were probably just trying in their hopeless, hamfisted way to do the best for her. We couldn't like her unless that side had been explored.

Gerry said that he thought the heroine should kill the senior executive by stretching some thread across the stairs, which would cause her to fall and break her neck. The heroine should have nail scissors ready and remove the thread while pretending to be concerned. Then the senior executive's job would be offered to the heroine and she would have plenty of money, get her own flat, and tell her parents to stop worrying about her.

Jane looked at Vincent, hoping that he would go next, but he gallantly waved a hand at her and encouraged her on. So Jane swallowed and told her story. It was about a woman who had spent her whole life since she was seventeen looking after her invalid mother. She had got no thanks, no recognition, and no recompense for it. Her brothers had been free as birds to find love and careers for themselves. They were married with children now, but they did not make her part of their families. The woman had met a lonely, neglected mother on social welfare, a girl hardly more than a child herself but who had a little baby, and eventually she decided to take them into her house and make a family for them all. . . . Jane stopped and looked around the little group. It was the usual silence.

"Well, it's a nice idea," said Clare, "but it doesn't go anywhere—remember they said there should be some turning point somewhere, where people do one thing or the other and that's what makes the story?"

"And what's the point of her being bitter about the awful brothers *now*?" Nancy asked. "If she's going to be bitter it should be when the old woman is alive, and she should make them each take their fair share. No use when it's all over. It's a bit feeble of her, wouldn't you think?"

Vincent said it was a hard premise to expect us to think that a woman who looked after a frail parent was somehow a loser. Most people did what they had to and got on with it. The reader wouldn't have any sympathy for the heroine—unless, of course, she made a really good home for the unmarried mother, but how could she do that if she had no job?

Gerry said that it should turn out that one of the brothers had murdered the mother, and the heroine should discover this and blackmail the brother into giving her a house.

Vincent cleared his throat and said that his story was about an alcoholic man who made everyone's life very anxious because he had long periods off the drink, and just when they were all relaxed he would suddenly go back on the drink again. And when he was sober he was the most wonderful, sensitive man in the world, and no one ever discovered why he went back on it.

They waited, but that was it.

Nancy said that, to be very honest, they should remember what had been said at the opening lecture. It wasn't up to us writers just to create mysteries: we had to solve them, too.

Jane said that in the end everyone gave up on mystery people: she had a regular guest in her house who was so secretive that it wasn't worth spending one more second of her life wondering about him, and the danger with Vincent's character was that people would give up on him in the book if there wasn't any outcome.

Clare said that we should know more about the alcoholic's family and whether they had tried to help him with tough love, or one of those ways of coping.

They hardly dared to look at Gerry, since they all knew it had been the boy's mother who was the alcoholic. Surely he couldn't have a murderous solution to this problem. It was too hurtful, too near home. But you could never tell at a writers' class.

Gerry said that maybe the alcoholic could have killed himself.

"But why would he do that?" Clare asked.

"Out of guilt—maybe he thought that he had done too much to the family already and they would be better if he was gone."

Vincent put out his hand and laid it on his son's arm. "She didn't do that, Gerry, it was an accident," he said, his voice very low.

The other three watched the tableau, hardly able to move.

Nancy didn't know where she got the courage to break the silence, but she spoke in a clear voice, as if calling them back to their surroundings. "Right—only Gerry left, what's your story?"

Gerry read out his typed pages about a boy who saved a man's life in a brawl and the man turned out to have magical powers. "I'll give you two wishes. But you must make them immediately," the man said. So the boy said he would like, for wish one, to go far, far away where no one had ever heard of him and where nothing reminded him of anything. And for wish two, he would like his father to meet someone nice and marry her and have a happy home of his own.

At that moment they were all called to pull their chairs around and hear the lecture.

The Tuesdays went on and none of the little group ever missed one meeting. They saw other tables where people had dropped out. They heard that one man had offended everyone by reading out pornography; and they heard that a steamy love affair had begun between two people at the table near the door and the woman in question was going to leave her husband. But they each wrote their ten pages every week and sent them by e-mail to the others on Monday nights so that they could come to the meeting with considered views.

Nancy's story changed. Her heroine came to realize how selfish the monstrous man was. She considered herself lucky to escape and found happiness in floristry, because the others said you should write about what you know. Jane's sad heroine became less sad and ran a B and B to make a home for the young mother and child. Clare's receptionist managed to implicate the senior executive woman in a financial scam. Vincent's alcoholic hero wrote a letter to his wife, explaining with episodes in his past why he was so frail. Gerry said he hoped that they didn't mind but he was going to write a nonfiction book, instead. He was going to make his theme Great Unsolved Murders. He really enjoyed them, and thought he could get a publisher interested.

They had lectures from authors, agents, publishers, theatrical producers, filmmakers, short story experts. They listened and they learned and they rewrote and came to take themselves seriously. By the end of the twenty weeks, they had admitted to other people that they were going to a writers' class, rather than keeping it a deep secret and pretending they were going to the cinema on a Tuesday night. They told their friends they were trying to write a book.

They all had a manuscript to show for it when the course

ended, and there was a little graduation party with wine to celebrate. Everyone was allowed to bring a guest or two.

Vincent and Gerry asked their neighbors, who had been kind
and supportive in the bad times. Jane asked Lilly to come with
her—her little daughter, Sophie, was over a year old now and
bright as a button. Nancy and Clare, who had become great pals
as the months had gone by, invited two fellows they had met at a
speed-dating evening, both of them perfectly nice men who
might well be part of the future but who equally well might not.

They had contemplated inviting the monstrous Ed so that he
could see how successful Nancy had become, and the appalling
series producer in the radio station so that she would hear all the
praise for Clare. But they decided that whatever else they had
learned in the writers' course, there was some very important
lesson about Moving On.

And when the ceremony was over, and they were having their
glasses of wine, they said that they would miss one another. They
could, of course, meet without the structure of the writing class
but it wouldn't be quite the same.

Then it turned out that Clare and Nancy were going to share
a big, sunny apartment they had found, so maybe they could
have the meetings there.

And further, it turned out that Vincent and Gerry were going
to sell the house where they had so many unhappy memories
and move in with Jane. They would help with the B and B
guests, take the wordless man for a silent pint now and then, and
be there for Lilly and little Sophie. So that was another place
they could go for their meetings.

So, they had written their books and that was a huge achievement—but they would still need support. There was all this business of submitting them and coping with rejection and
submitting them again. People often fell at that fence.

They would need one another more than ever, the people
whose lives had been changed already so much by the writing
class. . . .

I think you open with the action, introduce the two main characters.

—Maeve Binchy

Fay's New Uncle

Fay barely knew that she *had* an uncle. He hadn't come to her father's funeral; he had never gotten in touch with her and her brother, Harry, about anything at all. He had not been mentioned by anyone in the family.

So it was a total surprise when she got the letter from a district nurse way at the other side of the city asking if Fay could become involved in the matter of her uncle, Mr. J. K. O'Brien of No. 28 Chestnut Street. Mr. O'Brien was, at present, in the hospital and quite frail. He could be released only after a conference with a relative. Her name had been given as his one surviving relation.

At first Fay was about to say it was a mistake. She didn't know anyone on Chestnut Street, but then, her name was O'Brien, and on her mother and father's wedding certificate the best man's name had been written down as James Kenneth O'Brien. He could be her father's brother. But why get in contact now?

Fay was going to be twenty-five on her next birthday. What could explain the silence, coldness, and distance of a quarter century? She could ask her own brother, Harry, but he was away. He worked as a steward on a liner and was often gone for months at a time.

"Don't get involved, Fay; I beg you," her friend Suzanne advised. "You're too kind, too easygoing. This old guy will want you to clean his house, wash his underwear, do his shopping, all in the name of family. But where was he when you needed him?"

"I didn't need him," Fay said.

"Yes, you did, when they came and took the house from under you after your father died . . ."

"To be fair, there were a lot of debts and he hadn't paid the rent for a while," Fay said.

"Yeah, but a couple of hundred from Uncle James Kenneth would have helped."

"He might not have had it." Fay was defensive.

"If he lives on Chestnut Street he has it. Those houses are going up in value every day; remember that before you agree to do every hand's turn for him, Fay."

The girls had been longtime friends since school. They worked side by side in a dry cleaner's and lived on dreams that one day two handsome, rich American men would come in to have their elegant suits pressed. Their eyes would meet the eyes of Fay and Suzanne and the next thing would be dinner, almost the next thing would be marriage, and then there would be a life of ecstasy in Malibu.

But these men never turned up, so Suzanne and Fay shared a bed-sitter and saved some money every week to spend on a holiday in Ibiza in case the American movie men had taken their sharp suits there instead.

"I'll go and meet the nurse anyway," Fay said.

Nurse Williams was brisk and to the point. Mr. O'Brien had suffered a mild stroke; they needed to be sure that there was someone to keep an eye on him, to make sure that he took his medication, that he ate sensibly and looked after himself. Often it was a matter of poststroke depression, and if this were to be avoided they would need to be sure that he wasn't left to wallow around on his own.

"I don't think you understand, Nurse; this isn't a loving extended family. I never saw the man in my life, and he never remembered me or my existence until he needed me."

"He remembered you and agreed that we get in touch only after a lot of probing on our part and a great deal of reassurance that you would not be put out. We told him it would only be a formality."

"And wouldn't it? Be only a formality, I mean?" Fay asked.

"No, to be honest I think it would be more of a commitment, unless of course you could come to some arrangement with his neighbors."

"What are they like?"

"Well, Mr. O'Brien has bad luck in one way; the neighbors on either side are absentee landlords, people who own the property but rent their places, so the cast keeps changing. Some child down in number eighteen feeds his cat for him. I know that there's a nice, but fairly scatty hippie girl a bit farther down in twenty-six, and a rather earnest couple, fearful of any responsibility, in number twenty-five, but perhaps you could make further inquiries. . . ."

"What do they call him? James? Jim? Kenneth?" Fay asked.

"I'm afraid they call him 'Mr. O'Brien,' even us. It's what he wants," Nurse Williams said apologetically.

"Everyone?"

"Yes, everyone."

"Heigh-ho," said Fay.

"I'm Martin O'Brien's daughter, Fay," she said to the small man in the hospital bed.

"And where did he get a name like that for you?" the man said.

"He and my mother baptized me Mary Faith. I chose Fay."

"Huh," he said.

"And what do people call *you*?" she asked.

"You won't be here long enough for it to matter," the man said.

"Are you normally this charming to everyone, or is it only because I am your brother's daughter that you're making a special effort with me?" Fay asked.

"Very droll, very smart-arse," he said. "Like your mother."

"She needed to be both, to survive without a penny piece from Martin O'Brien. If it had no sense of direction and four weak legs Martin O'Brien put the housekeeping money, the rent, and the electricity on it. That was the system." Fay spoke without either bitterness or regret. It was the way things were.

"All I need is for you to sign me out; you can go your own way then."

"I'm sorry, but I have a very great sense of duty. I can't leave you alone to fall over and die."

"I haven't a notion of falling over and dying. I'm still a young man. I'm only seventy-four years of age, I'll have you know."

"You probably had no notion of having a minor stroke either. Can you let me have the keys? I'll go to your house with Nurse Williams, and we'll see what has to be done."

"You're not getting your hands on the keys to my house. . . ."

"Right, Mr. O'Brien, keep your keys, stay here, die in this hospital, let that child feed your cat till it dies. What do I care? I never gave you a day's thought in my life up to this, or you me. Why should things change now?"

"Are you normally as charming as this to everyone, or is it only because I'm your father's brother?" he asked.

There was a hint of a smile on both of their faces. She held her hand out.

"The keys, Mr. O'Brien, then?"

"It's Jim, Mary Faith," he said sheepishly.

"It's Fay, Jim," she said, and headed off for Chestnut Street.

"You'll have to be prepared for the house to be in a terrible state; sometimes they are." Nurse Williams had seen everything and knew it all.

"What do we do if it is?"

"Sanitation comes in if it's really terrible," Nurse Williams said, putting a handkerchief to her face as they opened the door of No. 28. But the place was fine, bare to the point of being sparse. There were few pictures on the walls; there were chairs that had never been comfortable and never been smart. A very small television set and a very big, old-fashioned radio stood beside each other on a table. Folded newspapers were piled high on a stool. Pale, faded, and many-times-washed tea towels were stretched out on the backs of chairs. There was no smell of food or decay. A very small fridge held just butter and margarine. A kitchen cupboard held a lot of tins and packets.

J. K. O'Brien of No. 28 Chestnut Street, no matter how upwardly mobile his address, did not live high on the hog. Fay thought of the nearby tenement where her mother had brought her and her brother up. It was very poor compared to this, but there was more life in every floorboard there than there was here.

What *had* the brothers quarreled over? Would Harry know? He was older; he might remember some row. Still, she must get down to the problem at hand.

"It's too big for one person, really. Would he be better to sell it and get a flat in a senior residence?" Fay asked.

"Of course, he'd be better doing that, but do you think he will?" Nurse Williams knew people held on to places. "No, he'll stay here until he drops."

"Should he live downstairs? He obviously doesn't use that sitting room at all. He could put a shower in the downstairs cloakroom."

"He'll do nothing, Fay; we have to do it before we let him out."

"But who'd pay for it? He doesn't look as if he's got very much. I've got nothing at all. . . ."

"If he leased the upstairs he'd get plenty, but then, who'd come and live with him, a complainer like that?" Nurse Williams tried to work it out.

"What was his job before he retired?"

"He worked in the post office, I think, it says on his records."

"He'd have to have a pension from that, so he'd be well able to afford the shower. Can we get someone in your outfit to put the money up for it first, and then tell him he has to pay for it?"

"I'd say that would be best. I'll get onto it from my end," Nurse Williams said.

Mr. O'Brien was outraged when he came home and heard that he would have to pay for the shower.

"If you were an ordinary person, Jim, you'd have all that money back in a couple of months just by leasing the upstairs as a flat. It would be paid for in no time."

"But who would I have upstairs?" He sounded aggrieved and very annoyed.

"Who indeed? I can't think of anyone who would stay here for five minutes," Fay agreed.

Jim O'Brien was confused. "But didn't you and that bossy nurse just tell me that the upstairs could bring in a great income?"

"Yes, indeed it could, but only to someone normal, someone who didn't grizzle about everything as soon as the door opened."

"You've trapped me," he cried.

"No, you see, Nurse Williams and I thought you *were* normal; most people are. That was the mistake."

"Why did you think that?"

"Because we didn't *know* you, Jim, and how you are over-interested in everyone else's life and behavior and oversecretive about your own. You've told me something about every single person on this street: how Kevin and Avril across in number two had a separation or a divorce, how Lillian in number five supports the whole household, how Miss Mack went blind, how Mitzi in number twenty-two had a romance outside her marriage years and years ago, how young Mandy's mother is a tramp over in number eighteen. . . ."

"Yes, but all those things are true," he blustered.

"The thing is, however, that none of them know anything at all about *you*," Fay said. "They don't know where you came from, what you did for a living, how long you've been here. They didn't know I was a relation; they thought I was a social worker."

"It's none of their business," he grumbled.

"I agree, but I *was* asked in by the hospital to help them work out whether you could live on your own, so I have to do my job and find out for them."

"And what have you found out?" He was anxious even though he was hiding it.

"That you'll be much better off living on the ground floor, and that I'll leave you my phone number for emergencies and I will call to see you every month. They'll let you stay here, Jim." She gave him a grin.

"You've been very good in ways," he said. "Badly brought up, of course, no manners or anything, but I suppose that was *her* fault. But still you came when you were needed. I'll say that for you."

Fay looked at him for a long moment without saying anything. Then she spoke.

"I don't know what you have against my mother. Harry and I have nothing but good memories of her. She loved your brother. She said she knew he was a gambler when she married him, so she had only herself to blame. She worked long, hard hours cleaning floors and stairways to keep food on our table and the rent paid."

"She was a vulgar woman who drank great big pints," J. K. O'Brien said, as if that settled it.

Fay looked at him in astonishment. "She worked her hands to the bone cleaning in order to pay for what she called her 'entertainment,' which was to take my father out on a Saturday and buy them two pints each in the local pub. She did that up to the week before she died. And he died a year later of a broken heart. Whatever you heard bad of her, it wasn't from your brother."

He was silent now.

"So, have we finished with each other now for a month, Jim? My telephone number at work is here on this piece of paper. I don't have a phone at home or a mobile."

"Where's home?" he asked suddenly.

The first question he had asked about her during all the days of negotiation about him and his health, his house and his future.

"I share a bed-sitter with my friend Suzanne, who works with me."

"How much does it cost?" he asked.

She told him.

"Is it very smart?" he wondered.

"No, it's quite shabby, as it happens."

"So, would you and Suzanne like to come and live here at a cheaper rent?" he offered.

She paused. "At no rent at all, it's a deal," Fay said.

"At *no* rent?"

"We'd keep an eye on you, do your shopping, tidy up the garden, and cook you Sunday lunch every week," she offered.

"I could get a fortune for upstairs. You and that bossy nurse as good as said so," he complained.

"You *could* get a fortune, if you were normal, Jim." Fay shrugged.

"Yes, well, that's as may be. And what do you and this Suzanne want to do with your lives? Or do you intend to go on working in this place forever?"

"What place, Jim?"

"The place you work in, a laundry or something, isn't it?"

He had almost remembered.

"A dry cleaner's, but you were close."

"Well?"

"Well, we hope we'll meet some gorgeous fellows who will marry us and take us away from all that steam and checking in of dirty garments." Fay managed a cheerful smile, as she always did when talking about what had to be endured.

"Where do you go to meet these people?" he asked.

"We don't meet them all that much, Jim. We *think* about meeting them, or we meet fellows who fall short of the mark in Ibiza every May."

"And what would you need to meet nice, smart fellows?" He seemed genuinely interested.

"I don't know, maybe be a bit smarter ourselves, brighter, you know, better educated, coming from a nicer kind of background, but since we can't be that, then we have to hope to be lively and knock them out that way!"

"Seriously, would you like to live upstairs?"

"Only if there's no rent, Jim, because if you're not going to be a normal landlord, we can't be normal tenants."

"But the cost of the bathroom downstairs!" he wailed.

"Will add hugely to the value of this house, Jim."

"When can you move in?" he asked.

"Suzanne will have to come and vet you first," she said.

"No, Fay, no. We're going to be clipping his toenails, feeding him porridge. *No!*"

"We have a fantastic flat for free. Come and see it."

"Nothing's for free. We know this."

"It's a posh address nowadays. Fellows will think we are something if we live on Chestnut Street rather than four flights up over a fast-food place. And we have a room each; think of what that might mean."

"Will you swear you won't let him interfere in our lives or tell us long, boring stories about the past?"

"I swear, because it will be easy," Fay agreed.

They established house rules. The girls could come in and go straight upstairs without having to check with Jim O'Brien each time. They were never going to tell him what time they were going out or coming back. They would make no loud noise upstairs or have parties without permission. They would cook a four-course

Sunday lunch for him every week and invite a neighbor or two on each occasion so as to set up a social life for him.

It worked amazingly well.

It meant that Jim O'Brien got invitations to other houses, which had never happened before. He came home full of tales about the various households he visited.

The girls suggested that they all buy between the three of them a washing machine and a dryer, and everyone learned to use them.

"Don't iron his shirts," Suzanne pleaded, so Fay taught him how to do them himself.

A couple of months later they bought a freezer between them. Jim liked that and made neat little labels for everything they put in it.

He asked them about their lives. He was interested in Fay's brother, Harry, the oceangoing steward.

"Have you met him?" he asked Suzanne.

"No, he's never really at home, you see. What a life!" She sighed.

"He'll come home one day; they all do. Home and settle— you might fancy him, you know."

"Why should I?"

"Well, if you're a pal of his sister that means you have something in common. That's how marriages often start."

"If you know so much, Jim, why didn't you marry?"

"I was stupid, kept thinking I had to have a nest egg, and by the time I did have a proper nest egg, I was old and set in my ways and it was no use to me," he said.

Jim O'Brien had a disconcerting habit of saying something simple and vulnerable when they expected him to be sour and putting people down.

When Harry came home next, Jim suggested that he form part of the Sunday lunch.

"Why did we never meet you when we were young, Jim?"
Harry asked casually, as they were doing the washing-up.

"I was half-cracked and took a dislike to your mother, quite
wrongly, as it turned out," Jim said.

"Oh, why do you think you did that?" Harry asked.

"Young fellas are eejits. Look at you yourself, now, and that
gorgeous girl under your very nose and you don't even notice
her," Jim said.

"What gorgeous girl?"

"Suzanne."

"She's a fine girl, all right." Harry nodded.

"So what are you drying dishes with me for? Why aren't you
asking her out?" Jim wanted to know.

"I'll kill him, your wonderful uncle. Kill him with my bare
hands," Suzanne hissed in the next room.

"Ah, go on, Suzanne, someone has to light a fire under
Harry." Fay laughed.

"Yeah, wait until he does something heavy trying to get a fellow for you," Suzanne grumbled.

But she combed her hair and put on a little more lipstick, and
when Harry suggested a walk along the canal she was ready to
show him the way.

"What are you doing for Christmas Day, Fay?" her uncle
asked, when the others were gone, and the two of them sat and
had a cup of tea together to end the Sunday ceremony.

"Why do you ask?" She was surprised.

"Well, it's not going to be a Sunday, you see, and I wonder,
would our arrangement extend to us having a Christmas dinner
together? I have enjoyed these Sunday lunches, you know. It's
worked out, from my point of view, very well."

"Sure, of course, Jim."

"And you . . . Do you think the arrangement is working?" He
seemed anxious for her approval.

"Certainly, I do."

"But you'd like a fellow of your own?" Now he sounded even more anxious.

"Well, someday, yes, Jim. Not today necessarily."

"But you're not rushing away? Not this minute?"

"No, of course not. Now that you've fixed my brother up with Suzanne, I'll sit on with you for a bit."

"Good."

They sat there amicably and an hour later a man knocked on the door. He was Billy Young, a financial adviser. He seemed delighted to meet Fay. Her uncle had spoken about her a lot, and had said she was a rock of sense.

"You're very pretty for a rock of sense," he said admiringly.

"Thanks, Billy," Fay said.

"Well, I'll get back to being an adviser," Billy said with a grin that broke her heart.

She went up to her room and remembered that she had to call Nurse Williams tomorrow for the regular check about whether it had worked out well or not. Had it been a success?

She lay on her bed and looked out over Chestnut Street. It had been a success. How dull that looked when written on an official form.

Before you begin [writing a story] you must
know the end.

— *Maeve Binchy*

Georgia Hall

Georgia had always been a leader.

Way back at school, she was the one with style. When Georgia decided to carry her schoolbooks wrapped up with a red ribbon, everyone else abandoned their schoolbags and satchels and got ribbons also.

It was the same when we arrived at university. She didn't appear to try too hard, but everyone wanted to do things her way. She read art history, always saying it was an undemanding thing to do, yet she was at the very top of her group. She had a little bed-sitter that she said was so terrible she couldn't imagine *anyone* wanting to visit it, yet every Friday there was a small drinks party there that people fought to be part of.

Georgia's hair always looked perfect. Compared to all the other girls, who had bad-hair days every day, Georgia looked as if she had just left an expensive coiffeur. Which she had, actually. She worked in a posh salon on Fridays, their busy day, and in return got a few tips, a good cut every month, and a shampoo and blow-dry every week.

She must have worked hard at her studies, because she was never seen out on weeknights, but on Fridays she played hostess to the college's finest. Saturday lunchtimes she was often seen in a pub on the river surrounded by college heroes, and she'd have a date at the best restaurants on Saturday nights.

It was hard to know whether people *liked* her or not. There was something calculated about her even then. Georgia never giggled or confided; she looked at you in a measured way with her big gray eyes, as if she were taking you in somehow. As though she were evaluating you, wondering was there something she could absorb from you for herself.

That's what I thought, anyway. But then obviously I wouldn't warm to Miss Georgia Hall.

Well, I mean, she took James, my boyfriend.

Of course, there are those who could and I'm sure *did* say that he wasn't forced to leave me for her; nobody put a noose around his neck or a gun to his head. James walked very willingly to Georgia's side that autumn.

One week he and I were running around catching falling leaves for good luck, and the next he was all dressed to kill in a new jacket, taking her to this expensive grill place that he and I had never been to and that he had often said was rather pretentious, because we couldn't afford it.

He handled it all very badly. "I suppose you've heard," he said awkwardly to me. Of course, I had heard. College was like a steamy goldfish bowl: everyone heard everything. But I would not let him have the satisfaction of knowing I had already been told.

"Heard what?" I asked. I was never Oscar material; I shouldn't even try to act.

"I know someone must have told you," he said. "I'm seeing Georgia."

"Of course, you see Georgia." I pretended to be dumb, forcing him to admit what I already knew.

"No, I mean *seeing*. In the sense of . . . going out with," he said.

"Oh," I said. It wasn't much of a response after all that manipulation.

"I'm sorry," James said foolishly.

"Well, if you're sorry you're going out with her—*seeing her*—then why do you do it?" I asked.

"No, I'm not sorry I'm going out with her," he snapped.

"So what *are* you sorry about?" I asked. It was childish, but then I was very hurt. I was entitled to some bit of revenge.

"I'm sorry for upsetting *you*, Moggie," he said.

I have to have this stupid name, *Moggie*. It's meant to be a pet name for Margaret. I realized later that I needn't stay stuck with it for life. I could have called myself something like Georgia. But by the time I realized that, it was too late.

"Me? Oh, I'm not upset."

"You're not?" He looked very relieved. Men are *so* simple at times.

"No, not at all."

He looked at me as if he had never seen me before.

I wondered what he actually did see. I'm not tall and graceful like Georgia Hall; I'm more dumpy, in fact, small and square and solid. My eyes look to me to be too close together. I always imagined they made me appear sinister, a bit like a criminal, even, though James had always said that I was silly to run myself down. My hair never looked as if it had *seen* a posh hairdresser, even if I did actually take it to one. It looked as if it had a life all its own and grew in different directions.

Unlike Georgia, I had no elegant clothes: no wispy scarves, no floaty skirts. Just the same jacket forever and a small variety of skirts and trousers. I was studying boring old economics, not lovely, ethereal art history.

No one in his right mind would blame James for his decision.

"You're amazing, Moggie, quite amazing," he said admiringly.

And I suppose I was. Amazingly angry.

Georgia was practically purring when I met her next. It was outside the dairy, where she was buying cheese for her Friday-evening soirée.

"James tells me you've been really super about everything,"

she said, and she rolled the words around before letting them out. I wanted to lift up a big wooden crate that was near us and break it over her head. I mean, it was a real urge, not just a passing fancy. But I beat it back.

It won't last, this romance, I told myself, *and then he'll come back on his knees to his Moggie. And I'll make him sweat a bit before I take him back.* I smiled at the thought.

"You look quite nice when you smile, Moggie," the patronizing Queen Georgia said.

There was an unspoken second half of the sentence, something like, *if only you got your teeth fixed,* or maybe, *if only you weren't so unacceptably tubby. . . .* She just left it hanging in the air, allowing me to fill in the blanks.

She can't win forever, I told myself, and smiled again.

But she did seem to be winning for a long, long time. Naturally she finished with James, who of course came bleating back, wondering if his Moggie could have it in her heart to forgive him. But actually, I didn't have it in my heart. I didn't want him anymore. He was no longer the great James who was going to change the world with me; he was a silly, vain man who liked the way the prom princess had smiled at him and brought him, temporarily, to a position of power in her court.

And we all got on with our lives. I got my degree in economics and joined a research foundation, where we did a lot of good work, and whether we changed the world or not I don't know, but we certainly dug around and found the facts and the statistics to help others change it. And James joined a rather right-wing firm of lawyers whose chambers handled a lot of corporate clients, the kind of people we once thought were the bad guys.

And Georgia Hall?

Oh, Georgia became famous.

She looked so good she was a natural for television, so they always had her on to talk about this art acquisition, or that discovery, or to sum up what somebody had done for art, and she spoke in a clear, unaffected voice, prefacing everything by saying, "It's only my opinion, now," which covered her if she was wrong about something and heaped great praise on her if she was right.

She helped to compile art books. It *was* suggested once that somebody she was collaborating with was going to sue her for taking the credit and doing none of the work. But that was all hushed up. Or possibly it was just gossip—I wasn't the only fly-ing bird whose wings had been singed by Georgia Hall.

Sometimes I used to tell people I had known her both at school and at university. But then I stopped. They always wanted details about her, and I realized how very little any of us had known her at all.

Did she have brothers and sisters? I don't know. Who were her real friends? Hard to say. People who mattered, possibly. That had always been a theme. Instead of the leading lights of the Debating Society, the Dramatic Society, or the rugby or the rowing clubs, Georgia's friends were now people in the arts, politicians, captains of industry, and even minor royals.

She had long left the little bed-sitter behind, and I heard or read somewhere that she had a *really elegant* London home. It figured.

She was *really elegant* everywhere: at the races, the opera, the Venice Biennale, some fund-raising dinner to keep a work of art in Britain.

I sound as if I were obsessing about her over the years. As if I watched her skyrocketing with some bitterness and a beady eye. But that's not true, as it happens. I was very busy and had little time to spend thinking about and envying the Girl Most Likely, as she had always been known. I had a life of my own.

The foundation where I worked got a lot of attention in the circles in which I would appreciate and care about such atten-tion, and I was headhunted by a small agency, where we did, though I say it myself, magnificent work on exposing inequalities of opportunity. We dealt with issues of class, education, race, religion, prejudice, and ignorance. Soon our work and findings were greatly in demand—from universities, investigative journalists, and local lawyers to campaigners, churchmen and politicians.

And in the agency I met Bob.

Everything changed after that. He had exactly the same dreams I did, the same belief that life was short and that whatever good had to be done must be done *now*. Bob was an eager, enthusiastic person who believed that people were basically good and all you had to do was to encourage them.

He seemed to like me a lot. *No—stop putting yourself down.* He loved me.

Bob loved me.

I used to ask him if there was something wrong with his eyesight when he told me I was beautiful. I didn't expect to be considered beautiful. I expected people to think I was basically all right, and I worked hard and I cared a lot and my heart was in the right place. But *beautiful*? No. That would be pushing things.

Bob would get quite annoyed. "Margaret, one more word and I swear I'm going to insist you wear a bucket over your head. You have beautiful, velvety brown, loving eyes—so can you shut up about them?" And I did, because in the great scheme of things the closeness of my eyes was quite a small factor.

And life went on well. My picture was often in the newspaper over various projects, and my parents were proud of me. They liked Bob and—after I had glared at them a lot—they stopped asking when they were going to see an engagement ring.

Bob and I lived in a small basement flat very near work. We often had work meetings in our own sitting room, and that was where we thought up a great scheme for the agency, which really worked well. It involved architects, planners, and builders giving instruction to volunteers about building houses in Africa. We got sponsorship from all kinds of people, and huge cooperation from schools. It really caught people's imagination.

And now even the arts world had become interested.

They were going to encourage ethnic design and murals for the projects to make them look less functional. Now, what we needed was someone who could be the public face of an appeal for sponsorship.

"We really need someone like Georgia Hall," Bob said. "If only we knew someone who could put us in contact with her."

I paused for a moment, before wondering aloud if she would even consider doing it.

"She would." Bob was definite. "I bet you anything she would."

All right. So I paused longer than I should have. But then my conscience took over.

I must not deprive this campaign of Georgia Hall just because I feared her and resented her and had definite history with her. No, I must tell Bob that I knew her from way back.

"You never said!" He was astounded.

"You never asked," I replied dully.

"My life is an open book to you, and now it appears you have all these secrets," he complained. "Is there anything else you never said? Are you married maybe? Are you a millionaire? Do you deal drugs?"

"Okay, Bob, I'll write the letter," I said.

She replied promptly. Very sorry, but too many commitments already . . . desolate to have to refuse . . . very worthy cause . . . wish it well. And a small handwritten P.S.

Imagine that being you, Moggie; I didn't recognize the name Margaret, thought it was a different person. But on looking at the pictures I should, of course, have known it was you. . . .

She didn't write that she would have known me anywhere. But she meant it.

A part of me was relieved. Oh, all right, be honest—I was *entirely* relieved that she wasn't going to do it.

Bob was undeterred. "No worries, I'll persuade her," he said confidently.

My stomach felt as if there were a lump of lead wedged in it as he set about getting in touch with Georgia Hall. All the skills and determination I had so much admired seemed hateful now as he forced his way into a fifteen-minute meeting with her at a television studio. That was all she could give him, he was told. That was all he would need, Bob said.

And he came back triumphant. She had agreed.

"She's very bright," he said admiringly. "Sharp as a tack is Georgia."

I looked at him wordlessly. The lead in my stomach had gone upward, toward my voice box. I couldn't speak. I wondered what Georgia saw when she looked at my Bob.

He was big and sandy-haired, with freckles on his nose. He had an eager, shambling way of expressing himself. He was wearing a corduroy jacket and a yellow open-necked shirt. He was so much *not* the kind of person she was always seen with, not suave or smooth or dissembling at all.

But perhaps Bob's transparent goodness was fashionable these days. Maybe Georgia—who had always been one to spot a trend—had seen the future. A familiar sense of dread came over me, paralyzing rational thought. Was I going to do the same this time? Pretend that it didn't matter, that I didn't care?

Had it worked the last time?

Well, in a way it had: James had come back. But by then I didn't want him back. That would not happen with Bob. James was a student flirtation; Bob was my mature and permanent choice. I didn't need the engagement ring or the semidetached house that my mother thought were the indications of security. I just wanted his love and shared vision.

And now it was all happening again. He had come back say-ing that Georgia was intelligent—*sharp as a tack*, whatever that meant. It proved conclusively that looks were the only thing that mattered in the end. Why had I been so blind for years?

I went to a hairdresser that day. An expensive place. He was a very pleasant man, the stylist. He told me that he and a few friends were going out as volunteers to build houses in Africa. He had recognized me from an interview in the papers.

I felt better after the cut. I told him that I thought I looked less of a fright than I had before. He laughed uncertainly, as if I had been trying to make a joke. I asked him what he would do if he had my small eyes, and he said that he thought my eyes and my heart were huge and had done a great deal for the world already; and I was so touched that my small eyes actually filled with big tears, and he had to give me a tissue.

Bob was meeting Georgia at her house to discuss details of the campaign.

I tried to concentrate on work all day, but it was hard. And it was hard even to continue breathing when he called later to say that Georgia was fixing something for them to eat in her house.

When he came home, the first thing he did was to admire my hair.

"It's lovely," he said simply.

Pure guilt, I assumed. But I smiled a feeble smile and listened while he told me how quick she was and how streetwise and a dozen other good things he seemed to have noticed about her.

She was coming to the office the next day; she wanted to meet the team, and she would go to Africa next week.

"That will cost a bit, knowing the style she'll be used to," I said sourly.

"No, she's making a point of paying her own way," he said. He was under her spell just like all the others. Suddenly I knew why witch doctors existed and still exist in different forms—agony aunts, counselors, lifestyle gurus. People who will help us to find a stronger spell, better magic to vanquish the rival.

Bob was still talking about her. He seemed to have noticed nothing of her house, only Georgia and every word she said.

"She spoke very well of you," he said.

How *dare* she talk about me before she replaced me. I found myself contemplating killing her when she came into the office the next day. I might ask her to look out of the window and then elbow her through. Or maybe just push her down stairs. It didn't make me feel any better, but it did tire me out and I was asleep in no time.

I dressed in my best outfit the next day and put on a serious layer of makeup—but, of course, you could never second-guess Georgia Hall. She was in blue jeans and a floppy sweater, and she had her shiny blond hair tied back with a rubber band. Her gray eyes were enormous as she listened to everyone on the team describing the work that was being done in an African township.

She appraised me as I came in. I felt like a shabby piece of artwork that she was about to expose as a fake.

"Well, Moggie, what a wonderful place for you to work," she said.

The others looked at me enviously. They thought she was magical. They hadn't noticed that she left hanging the rest of the sentence, which went something like, *considering you are so hopeless and dumpy and stupid. . . .*

And as I knew she would, she found Bob the most wonderful part of this wonderful place she had come to.

"What a performer!" she said, when he had finished speaking about the work that was being done with African communities. "He should have his own television show," she purred, "he's so very powerful."

I felt dizzy. It would happen in front of my eyes, and I was powerless to prevent it. Bob was not a performer; he believed everything he said. But under her corrupting gaze he would *become* a performer. Everything he had worked for would be thrown away.

I didn't kill her. I was just too tired and sad. I suppose I worked on autopilot for the day, which seemed to last for about eighteen months. I thought it would never end. And as I had predicted, Bob took her home to go over all that she had learned so that she would be ready for the interview at the airport as she left the following morning for Africa.

I waited for him to telephone me to say that he would be going with her, to *organize* things, to oversee it all. I waited patiently. He wouldn't actually say that he had to go *in order to hold her hand*, but that was exactly what it would be.

When the phone rang, I was almost ready for it.

But it was Georgia. He had actually asked Georgia Hall to ring me. He couldn't even face telling me himself. He knew how upset I would be; he had asked her to do it.

"Oh, *Moggie*," she said, her voice silky. "You are *so* lucky, Moggie, but then I always envied you. Always, from the very start."

"Yes, I suppose you did." She clearly expected me to bluster and say, *Nonsense, Georgia, you were the one we all envied and still do*, so, of course, I decided to go along with the mad premise that I was the object of admiration.

"You always had everything: parents who cared about you and came to school plays and knew how you were getting on, little brothers who thought you were great. And at university you had marvelous friends, real people, not just *poseurs*. Now you have real work with real values, not just posturing, like I have to do."

So that was the route she was going to take. I had always had a charmed life, so I should be prepared to give up Bob without a squeak because poor Georgia had nothing.

"So?" My voice was glacial.

"So Bob asked me to call you to say he's on his way home but he'll stop to get takeaway. Now that's what I call real devotion."

She was such an actress. If I hadn't known better, I'd have believed her and thought she truly did envy me, but I knew he would be back shortly with the food and that when we had opened the bottle of wine he would tell me that he needed to go with her.

When he came back, he was full of plans for the press conference tomorrow at the airport and how he hoped Georgia wouldn't make it into a three-ring circus.

"Maybe it's just me, maybe I bring out the worst in her, but honestly, she's such hard going, isn't she?" he said.

I hadn't an idea what he meant.

"I know we should be sorry for her, really," he argued with himself. "But it's such a fragile existence, thinking entirely of herself. She has to be center-stage every step of the way: what people will think of her, what she should wear, how she should sound knowledgeable about tribal art that she doesn't really know inside out. Whether it might mean she will get an honor, and if so would it be an MBE or an OBE? She would drive anyone insane. No wonder you never mentioned her to me."

He had opened the wine. He had said nothing yet about leaving with her tomorrow. But surely he would; he was only softening me up by telling me how feeble she was. Too feeble to go on her own.

But still he didn't say it, and we finished our food, talking on about the media attention she would draw to it all and how tragic it was that we needed gimmicks like this to get good people to do good things.

And then he said, "In an entire evening of self-absorption and self-pity she said only one thing of any interest. She said she had always envied *you*, that you were very sure about everything—what you wanted to do, that your family and friends would always be there, in your belief that the world could be a better place. She said she had lived by image alone, and it wasn't necessarily the right star to follow."

"She revealed all that about herself? She must really think highly of you!" I was astounded.

"Well, I had her number from the start, of course. I could see her image was the most important thing to her. That's how I got her to agree to it in the first place. I told her that her image was slipping. It was too brittle, too uncaring, always being seen at the races, the first nights, the parties. It was time for something more substantial, time she got involved in something—and she bought it."

He smiled gleefully.

"We'll get more support for the project, more houses built, and a higher profile, but, goodness, at what a cost. Come here and give me a hug to cheer me up."

I hugged him, and over his shoulder I caught my reflection in the mirror. Maybe it was the light, but perhaps I did after all have beautiful, velvety brown, loving eyes. . . .

*We must be interested in the hero or
heroine. . . . We have to care enough about the
people to follow them through to the last page.*
                                   —Maeve Binchy

The White Trolley

It had been a long, hard year running the shop. Too many very
early mornings, too many late nights. A lot of anxiety about introducing new lines. But the Patels had gotten it right. It was
Christmas Eve, and they knew that they had more than justified
Uncle Javed's hopes for them. It was up and running now, their
own place, in the middle of city offices. A place where they had
the courage to stock much more than the usual sandwiches and
fast food for office lunchers. They had even opened a gift section
with small electronics, unusual stationery, little leather goods,
and gadgets of every kind.

The other shopkeepers had shaken their heads and said they
were mad. But the Patels were newly married and fired with
ideas, gently encouraged by the watchful Uncle Javed. The
young couple had a gut feeling about the kind of service city
workers needed, and now, as they finally prepared to close for
the Christmas holidays, the Patels stood and watched proudly as
their most successful venture, white trolleys overflowing with
carefully packed goods, waited in line to be collected.

These were goods that had been bought in the lunch hour or
during the day, when customers had been able to slip away from
their offices. Each trolley had a name written on it with a big felt

pen on cardboard. The customer showed the receipt and then pushed the trolley out the door. There was a chorus of greetings and good wishes, and the Patels watched as a hundred different Christmases left their shop in trolleys. Uncle Javed congratulated the Patels, remarking that there were many new faces among the regular customers.

Mr. Patel was talking to one of the regulars when Uncle Javed gave the trolley marked s. WHITE to a young, anxious-looking woman with long hair falling into her eyes. Mrs. Patel was outside in the cold, pointing toward a bus stop and giving directions, when Uncle Javed gave another trolley marked s. WHITE to a stooped man with sad eyes. Then, under Uncle Javed's mischievous gaze, the young couple closed their store and took the first proper rest they had known for over a year.

Sara White pushed the trolley to the van, where Ken waited patiently. There was someone like Ken in every office, a man who didn't drink, who didn't seem to have any real life of his own, not one that he talked about, anyway. But who was always there, ready to help. It had become a tradition that Ken drove people home after the Christmas Eve office party. He piled all the carrier bags into the back of the van and returned the trolley to the little line. His three other passengers were still singing cheerfully as he dropped each of them at their homes, and they seemed reluctant to leave.

Only Sara was sober and silent as she sat beside him in the front seat.

"You must have bought up the whole shop," Ken said to her.

"Well, it's going to be a difficult Christmas this year. I want to make it different for them, not too traditional and all that," Sara said, and looked out the window at the crowds making their way home in the rain.

Sara's husband had left home in the springtime. Quite unexpectedly, apparently. She had spoken little of it in the office, but some of the girls had told Ken that she cried a lot and always expected that he would phone and say he was coming back.

"I'm going to make them Thai curry tomorrow. They'll like that, and it won't be sort of reminding them, you know."

"I know," Ken said, even though he didn't.

He helped her into the house with the carrier bags. Last year there had been a tall, thin man in a red sweater called David opening the door and, taking the bags for her, he had invited Ken in to have a drink. This time two children opened the door.

"You're very late," the girl said disapprovingly.

"I suppose it was all stupid games and things at the party," the boy said.

"You remember Ken." Her voice was bright. Too bright.

"Yeah," said the girl.

"Hi," said the boy.

Ken said good night sharply. No, thanks, he didn't want to come in. He wished everyone a very Happy Christmas.

"Well, now," Sara said.

"Well?" said Adam, who was thirteen and had come to the end of a bad day. All his friends seemed to be having proper Christmases, with presents and relations and trees and parties. Adam didn't know what he would do if his mother said once more in that false sort of tone she spoke with sometimes that it was just a day. . . . "That's all Christmas is when you come to think of it, just a day."

"Well?" said Katie, who was twelve and missed her father with a dull sort of ache that never went away. Things would never be all right again. When they saw their dad he just sighed and groaned and cast his eyes up to heaven about their mother. Her mother couldn't speak of Dad without shaking and trembling and talking about that woman and all the trouble she had caused. Adam and Katie didn't talk about Dad at all. It was easier.

But nothing was easy at Christmastime. They watched as their mother's false smile tried to reach her eyes and didn't succeed.

"Well," she said again, "let's see what we've got here." And very slowly she began to unpack onto her kitchen table the entire Christmas shopping list of a Mr. Stephen White. His credit card receipt was in one of the bags. A man who liked wrapped sliced white bread, and tins of peas and two portions of frozen turkey breast. A man who had bought ten tins of cat food, and four horrible, horrible little packages of talcum powder and soaps with MERRY YULETIDE written on them. Unbelieving still, Sara opened bag after bag. Everything she hated most in the world was unfolding before her. Packet stuffing for a turkey! Could this man have intended to put some dry packet stuffing in a frozen breast of turkey? There were tins of made-up custard; there were convenience foods like she had never known. Things you boiled in a bag; things you stewed in a packet of sauce. Sara's eyes were round in horror.

Her face began to crumple, and for the first time since their father had left, the children saw that their mother was about to cry. Adam and Katie looked at each other in amazement. She had never cried when Dad had walked away and gone off to live with that strange Mrs. Hunter, the woman with the greasy hair and the long, droopy cardigan. And here she was now about to collapse because of something to do with the shopping.

Sara fought back the tears. She could not let herself go now, now of all nights. But it was eight o'clock on Christmas Eve. Some half-witted man called Stephen White in some other part of the city had the beautiful soft leather handbag she had bought for Katie, the tiny CD player with the ten carefully chosen discs that she had found for Adam. The pure silk scarf that would go with Katie's green eyes, the camera that Adam had always wanted.

This man, who ate white bread and frozen turkey breasts, would have all the lemongrass and black olives, fresh limes and coriander. He would have the fresh prawns, the designer salad ingredients, the superb cheese. Even if there *were* any other stores open now, which she doubted, Sara couldn't afford to buy anything else. She had spent half a month's salary in Patels', and they with their happy marriage and successful business had managed to ruin everything for her. Because of their incompetence she was going to have to serve this man's revolting food for Christmas. Or they would eat nothing at all.

She didn't deserve to be let down like this. She had worked so very hard and fought so very bitterly to have the children to herself this Christmas. She didn't want them going anywhere near David and that appalling Marjorie Hunter, who looked as if she never washed her face or combed her hair.

David said it wouldn't be Christmas for him if he couldn't see the children at least for a little bit of the day. He had offered all kinds of things: he could collect them, he could visit them for an hour, he could send a taxi for them. He would be lonely, he said.

"You should have thought about that when you left them," Sara had said crisply.

"Please, Sara." He had actually begged her.

"How could you possibly be lonely, David?" Sara had said. "You have the lovely Marjorie Hunter to entertain you." And he had hung up then. Defeated.

She saw both the children staring at her. Worried.

"Do you want us to put the shopping away?" Katie asked.

"I'll open the freezer," Adam offered.

"This isn't the shopping," Sara sobbed, her shoulders heaving. "This isn't anyone's normal shopping; it's the shopping of a madman." And with her head between the tins of cat food and the packets of instant whipped mousse, Sara White wept all the tears that the children had never seen her shed in this, the worst year of their lives.

They were entirely at a loss. For month after long month coping with Dad leaving had been brittle and tense. Katie had tried to talk. She had sat on her mother's bed and begged her to tell her what had happened. But she got no answer. Only that strange, unnatural laugh that didn't sound at all like her mother.

Adam had wondered was it because he had gotten a bad school report? Could that have had anything to do with it? But again that laugh; he wasn't to be so silly to think that a bad report could make a father leave home.

They couldn't understand why she had never cried. The children could not understand that their mother was tormented with her own desperate questions, and the person with the answers had simply walked away.

Katie and Adam hardly dared to touch the weeping woman with her head down on the table in the middle of this perfectly ordinary-looking shopping. But, tentatively, Katie touched her mother's shoulder. Adam went and got a great lump of paper towels for her to dry her eyes. Gradually Sara sat up and looked at them. She blew her nose loudly and gave each of her children a squeeze.

"It's just the last straw, you see," she explained.

They didn't see.

"I wanted it to be special for you," she said humbly.

They huddled together and talked. She told them how much she loved them and how hard she had fought for them this Christmas. And now there were only terrible, terrible things to cook, and all their lovely presents gone forever to this madman.

"I don't mind these things," said Katie. "You don't have to cook with them; we'll do it." Katie waited for her mother to protest. But Sara took one glance at the alien food on her table and sighed heavily. Adam held his breath and followed his mother's gaze. At least she had stopped crying.

"This stuff's easy to cook," he boasted. "And we'll find the madman after Christmas and get our presents back."

His mother touched his cheek. The small gesture surprised Adam, and he felt happy. For the first time in months, he and his sister did not seem like some impossible burden their mother had to suffer alone.

Warily, Sara watched her son and daughter play with the garish items that had been bought by Mr. S. White. The tins and packets were being tossed carelessly between Adam and Katie, their faces getting increasingly excited as they invented elaborate names for the dishes on their Christmas Day menu; a meal of sorts seemed possible, Sara conceded. She looked at her children, both ridiculously pleased with themselves, and she felt blessed. They deserved their presents, and she knew, she had always known, what they really wanted for Christmas.

"Would you like to call your dad?" she asked gently. The children looked at her; their shoulders sagged slightly and they avoided her eyes. "You can invite him to your lunch," she added softly.

"Only if he brings some food and our presents," said Katie too brightly.

"Don't be silly! He wouldn't come without *her*!" Adam tried to hide his frustration, but recently their lives had become so complicated.

"Daddy *could* bring her," said Katie hesitantly.

A furtive look passed between Katie and Adam; they hardly dared to hope.

Sara studied the shopping of Mr. S. White with open suspicion. "Do you really think you can manage this lot?"

Two eager faces beamed back at her.

"Easy," said Adam confidently. Katie nodded her agreement.

Sara sighed. Her children were right, she thought: it was easy, and she went to the telephone. "I will have to warn Daddy . . . and . . . Marjorie," she said, and smiled at the two impish faces, "that it will be a light and very uncomplicated lunch."

They say that when beginning a story you should always try to catch people at some interesting juncture of their lives.

—Maeve Binchy

The Feast of Stephen

Stephen White had always liked the Patels, who ran the great shop near his office. They were such a hardworking couple, and yet they always had time to have a few words.

Mrs. Patel had once advised him what to take to a colleague who was in the hospital. Stephen White had been going to buy her chocolates, but the busy little woman in her sari said that she thought a packet of cards with envelopes would be better, and then if he were to get her a book of stamps as well that would be perfection.

It had indeed been a highly acceptable gift. The woman in the hospital bed had been surprised at receiving something so thoughtful.

Foolishly Stephen told her it was the suggestion of the woman in the minimarket. It seemed to diminish the gift but Stephen was such a fair-minded person, he didn't want to take credit for an idea that was not his own. He had always been that way. Not pushy enough, his father had said, but then nobody was pushy enough for Stephen's father, who had eventually pushed himself into a situation where he was prosecuted for fraud.

Never stood up for himself, his sisters had said, and Wendy, the wife who he thought had loved him, had left him because she said that he would never light a fire under anyone, himself included.

Stephen hadn't known that he was meant to light fires under anyone. It hadn't been part of any original deal. He thought you went out and worked hard and earned money and stood behind other people in queues and waited your turn. He didn't know a new system had come in, where you were meant to have a confrontation about everything, and not to back down and not to lose face.

And this, of course, was why he was in this situation just before Christmastime.

Redundant. Fired. He no longer had a job.

His boss had been embarrassed.

"There's no easy way to say this, Stephen, and no good time of year to say it, either," she had begun.

He had looked at her blankly.

"But of course you must have seen it coming," she went on.

Stephen hadn't seen it coming. And not on Christmas Eve.

Earlier that day the Patels gave him his receipt and put his trolley away, having written S. WHITE in large letters on cardboard for when he would collect it later.

They were really a highly efficient pair; they deserved their success. At that time, of course, Stephen thought he was a man with a job and a future.

Not so when he came back after the news of the afternoon. This time he was like someone on autopilot. It was his first Christmas alone; he just had to pick up his shopping and face it. For the last two years since Wendy had left him he had gone to his brother's house.

But they played a lot of games there, things you had to be quick-witted about. It wasn't easy or relaxed.

This year Stephen had thought he would make his own Christmas dinner, get two frozen turkey breasts—one looked so sad. And you never knew who might join you.

George in the office had said he might stroll by. Not a definite arrangement or anything, but just a possibility. Stephen had wanted to be prepared. He would get nice, easy foods, like tins of custard and packets of mince pies. And some packet soups and stuffings, things you just had to add a little water to.

Small gifts for the ladies in the flats near him; they would like talcum powder and matching soap, he thought.

He bent sadly over the trolley and brought it out to his car.

He unpacked bag after bag, all of them with SEASON'S GREET-INGS written on them. He stacked them neatly in the trunk. He knew that he had bought far too much. George wouldn't stroll by, not tonight or tomorrow. You didn't stroll to the house of a man who had just been sacked. There would be nothing to say.

Grimly Stephen continued unloading his supplies. But he didn't really look at them. Otherwise he would have realized he had the wrong trolley. He was a person of regular habits and permanent rituals. Normally he would have put anything for the freezer on one side of the trunk and covered it with a rug for greater insulation. But tonight he didn't make any distinction. And he headed out into the rainy night with tears on his face. Tears of failure as he drove the contents of Sara White's trolley to the small flat where he had lived since he and Wendy had sold what was always called the marital home.

Back at the office the party would be in full swing. He had always, in his quiet way, enjoyed it on other Christmas Eves. He found a background from which to observe it all; it had been good-natured, if a little silly.

But this year they would all have been sympathizing with him, assuring him he would get another job in no time. Better let them speculate about him behind his back, wonder how poor Stephen was taking it all.

He would show up after Christmas and tidy things up. He had been told that he need not leave until sometime that suited him early in the New Year.

Stephen opened the first package and discovered prawns in their shells. Well, now, he thought, the Patels were not as efficient as he had thought; they must have included a bag from someone else's trolley. Still, it was easy to do. He looked at the prawns, interested; they were so prehistoric . . . almost like dinosaurs, really. He wondered who could possibly cook and eat such things. Then the next bag had a leather handbag and a green scarf. There were jars of olives, strange crusty bread with an herby smell. It took Stephen White five whole minutes to realize that he had none of his careful shopping, that, in fact, he had been given totally the wrong trolley.

But it had his name on it back in the store, which was long closed now. And surely his credit card receipt must be in one of the bags. He rooted around to find it, and there it was behind a miniature CD player that must have cost a fortune. But it was for Sara White; that was what she had signed.

Some crazed woman who must, by the amount of her bill and the look of her trolley, run an exotic restaurant and quite possibly a gift shop. What must she be thinking in some other part of the city as she looked for all these entirely inappropriate things that she had presumably assembled for herself and her family?

And how was he going to find her? The credit card people wouldn't reveal her address. The Patels would be locked up and gone away.

Suddenly Stephen felt very tired and sad. He sat at the kitchen table loaded with such unexpected things. A big tear splashed down on the coconut milk. He would never find this Sara White in the phone book; there was no point even in looking—she might be there under her husband's name.

His Christmas was ruined because this *stupid, stupid* woman couldn't take the right trolley. But that wasn't really why the tear had fallen. The food didn't matter. Stephen White sat weeping in the kitchen on Christmas Eve, because at the age of forty-eight he was unemployed and his wife had been gone for two years and he had nobody and nothing to live for.

There was a loud banging on the door.

Stephen brushed his face and went to answer it. It was George from the office, with a bottle of wine and possibly quite drunk already.

"I was strolling by," said George, who lived in another part of the city entirely and had made the detour out of solidarity with the man who had just been sacked.

George was amazed at all the food. He examined all the ingredients.

"Imagine that. Well, I don't believe it! You were going to make a Thai curry," he said, full of admiration.

"Was I?" Stephen was bewildered.

"I must say I do admire you, Stephen. A few of us wondered if you would be all right; you looked a bit gray this afternoon. . . . Wait until I tell them you were having a party."

"A party?"

George laughed easily as he drew the cork from the bottle of wine he had brought with him.

"Well, don't tell me you were going to eat all this yourself! When's it going to start?"

"I don't know," Stephen said.

It was all becoming increasingly unreal sitting here with George from the office drinking a full-bodied red wine at a table covered with some woman's fancy shopping, having been sacked from his job.

"What time did you tell them?" George wanted to know.

"I didn't tell them," Stephen said.

George wasn't bothered by that. He refilled his glass.

"Well, they could come anytime then," he said in a brisk and businesslike way. "Come on, Stephen, we'd better get our skates on, start frying the mushrooms and onions."

"But what for?" Stephen begged.

"Well, as a base. Then we fry the chicken, stir in the green paste and the coconut milk. . . ."

"We can't do this. . . ." Stephen was hoarse with fear.

"Well, of course, if you want to make the green curry for the prawns, well, that's fine; we'll do a red one for the chicken."

"But the people! I haven't asked anyone!" Stephen cried.

"Well, definitely skates on then, Stephen, we'd better go around asking them."

And in front of Stephen's horrified eyes, George from the office, carrying a glass of red wine and most certainly under the weather from the office party, went across the corridor and banged loudly on the door of Mrs. Johnson, pillar of the residents' association, undoubtedly the most difficult woman in the entire building.

Stephen had bought her some talcum powder and a matching soap, hoping to get into her good books so she wouldn't glare at him quite so much.

But, because of that appalling Sara White, whoever she was, he had *no* talcum powder for Mrs. Johnson; he had only an inebriated colleague—well, ex-colleague—hammering on the woman's door. Stephen felt slightly faint. And closed his eyes. When he opened them, he saw to his amazement that Mrs. Johnson seemed to be having a perfectly normal conversation with George. She was even asking him what kind of bottle she should bring.

"Anything at all, really," George was saying. "Adds to the excitement."

George said he would be back shortly; he had now gotten the names of other residents from Mrs. Johnson, and everyone would assemble in about an hour. They should have everything ready by then.

Stephen sat down beside the wreckage of the table and the greatly reduced wine bottle. This just couldn't be happening. It was all a dream; he had fallen asleep and dreamed it all. That was it. Then he heard George's voice booming downstairs and excited cries coming from that quiet couple in No. 16, who hardly ever looked up from the pavement to talk to you. George had asked these people to Stephen's house and was planning to cook all Sara White's insane shopping list for them.

The phone rang.

He hardly felt strong enough to answer it, but he picked it up. It was a woman's voice.

"Stephen?" she said.

"Yes," he said bleakly.

"Stephen White?" she sounded doubtful.

"Oh, is that Sara?" he asked with real warmth in his voice. "I'm so glad you rang."

Now this terrible woman could come and take all her stuff and give him back what he wanted, what he had bought, in fact.

"No." The voice sounded disappointed. "No, it's Wendy, actually. Who's Sara?"

"Wendy!" He couldn't have been more surprised.

"Yes, well, season of goodwill and all that. I just thought I'd ring to ask how you are."

"I was sacked today, as it happens."

"Best thing that could have happened to you," Wendy said. "You were always too good for them, but you'd never leave. Now you can do something you'd enjoy."

"Yes, well . . ." Wendy was always very positive, no challenge too difficult for her.

"Are you depressed and moping about it alone at home?" she asked.

He thought for a moment. Wendy couldn't be doing all that much herself if she had called him.

"No, actually I'm having a party shortly," he said.

"A *party*!" Wendy couldn't believe her ears.

"Yes, Thai curry, chicken and prawns," he said proudly.

"Well, good for you." She sounded grudging and astonished, and a little lonely.

"You're very welcome. I'd love to see you again, Wendy," said Stephen White to his ex-wife.

"In about an hour's time, then, that would be great," she said.

And George came back to say that it was shaping up as a fine party list, but they should really think of getting their skates on, and as he had collected five different bottles already, perhaps they should open one for the sheer conviviality of it all.

Finding your voice . . . means finding a way to write that is comfortable for you. It's finding the method to tell your story that seems natural.
—Maeve Binchy

Dusty's Winter

She had been born in 1966, when Dusty Springfield was top of the pops, so that was what they called her. It was almost impossible to believe that her mother had once listened to pop records and cared enough about them to name her only daughter after a female vocalist. Especially since her mother was nearly forty at the time and had not expected a little Dusty, or a little anything, to join their nice, neat family of two boys who were eleven and ten. Nowadays the family was much too sensible to call their children after pop stars. She couldn't imagine her brothers choosing names like Bono or Meat Loaf. Yet that was what it must have been like. A bit racy, really, not in step with their nice, safe, ordinary life. Dusty often wondered what she would fill in if she were asked to do a questionnaire about her childhood.

Happy? Yes. Or sort of happy. Not unhappy, let's say, yes—that would be more like the truth. She would have to put "not unhappy," and yet anyone who read that as an answer would say that poor child must have been wretched or frightened. That certainly was not the case. Her father had gone out every morning at ten past eight and had come home every evening at ten to seven. He worked in the office.

They weren't poor but they weren't rich.

Dusty's mother worked mornings in a café nearby. It involved making the open sandwiches for lunch and piping whipped cream onto cakes, as well as serving. It was much more than just waiting tables. When Dusty was a baby she was wheeled there in her pram and put to sleep out in the back with Lionel, the son of the owner, and Sergio, the son of the Italian woman who did the washing up.

Dusty didn't know she was sleeping beside Lionel and Sergio. They were in their own prams with their own mothers coming to coo over them.

During the school holidays she remembered her brothers, Daniel and Harold, coming into the café with their friends. But they didn't come out to the back where Dusty, Sergio, and Lionel were growing up in a room that had become a nursery, with pictures on the walls and toys. In many ways Sergio and Lionel were really her brothers. Daniel and Harold were grown-ups.

By the time Dusty was five and in school, Daniel had a girl-friend. And a year later there was a terrible row at home. Dusty didn't know what it was about, but it had something to do with her mother being at work and not being at home to keep an eye on things. They told her to go and play and not to interrupt them.

Dusty went down to the café. Sergio and Lionel were always glad to see her. She didn't normally go there anymore. And it involved crossing two main roads. Her mother didn't like her making the journey on her own. But that day nobody would have noticed if she had gone down the road in a parachute.

Her father had come home from the office in the middle of the day. He kept calling her mother "Jean" in a sharp, angry tone. Normally he called her "dear." And Daniel had been crying, which was extraordinary. Grown-up men of seventeen didn't cry.

She told it all to Sergio and Lionel, and they tried to guess what it might be. But they couldn't think of anything, so they stopped guessing and played Happy Families. When her mother came to collect her, Lionel's mother said that they were all playing Happy Families, and her mother had started to cry in the café in front of everyone.

And shortly after that, Mother stopped working in the café, and so Dusty's mornings during the holidays were spent at home. Mother cleaned a lot and got cross if any mud came into the house. And if Sergio and Lionel came to play, there was always a bit of trouble about kicking up the grass.

Dusty would love to have played in Sergio's house or down at the back of the café with Lionel, but her mother said she had learned one lesson, and the other children would not be let out of her sight.

At school, Dusty made other friends, proper friends, girls who told one another secrets and had plans and got ready for parties. And they had a marvelous teacher called Miss Howe whom they all loved. They made up stories about rescuing Miss Howe from a burning house or from a muddy river or from a savage dog. They dreamed of inviting Miss Howe back for tea. She lived not far from Dusty. Perhaps Dusty could ask her. But Dusty thought not.

Miss Howe was full of excitement and stories about history. Miss Howe could make you feel you were there when the wooden horse arrived in Troy, or when Hannibal came over the Alps. She would find it very dull at home, where people said, "Pass the salt, please," and not much else. Meals were pretty silent. Miss Howe wouldn't enjoy that.

Daniel and Harold sort of looked into the plates and wished for the meal to be over. Dusty chattered on and they all looked at her fondly, but nobody made any effort to keep the conversation going, so she began to be silent also, thinking about funny things at school, or Sergio and Lionel at the café.

If anyone had asked if she was a lonely child, Dusty would have said, "Heavens, no." And then, "Well, not really lonely."

There were plenty of people about. But there wasn't anyone whom you could talk to fully. Friends went home to their own families and, as she grew up, she saw less of Sergio and Lionel, which was a pity, but it was the way things were.

Sergio's father had done something bad. Sergio didn't know what it was, but it involved his mother's brothers coming over from Italy, and big arguments. Now his father was not allowed to come home.

Lionel knew all about it. He said Sergio's father had been playing with another lady.

"Why shouldn't he play with ladies?" Dusty asked.

"I don't know," Sergio said. "He doesn't play much with me at home. Maybe he just likes to play with other ladies."

Lionel shook his head. "No, that's not the way it works. You're not meant to play with other ladies, only one lady."

"That's a big dull," said Sergio.

"It's what they fight over," Lionel said sagely.

"Nobody's playing with ladies in our house, but they do seem to be fighting quite a bit. Especially with Daniel," Dusty confided.

"Ah, that's because of Daniel's baby," said Lionel.

"But he doesn't have a baby," Dusty said.

"He does, too."

"Well, I've never seen it. It's not in his room."

"No, silly, he doesn't have it. The girl has it."

"I thought you had them only if you lived together." Dusty was very confused.

"You have to live together only for a bit, a very short bit."

"I don't think that's true. I'll ask."

"Don't. I'll get into trouble," Lionel pleaded.

But Dusty asked anyway. "Does Daniel have a baby anywhere?" she asked, as they were setting the supper table. She remembered it for the rest of her life. Everyone seemed frozen where they were, like a game of statues.

Eventually her mother said in a strangled voice, "Where did you hear that, Dusty?"

Dusty decided to protect Lionel. "Everyone at school says it."

Daniel's face was white.

"Now, Daniel," said their mother. "Now, do you believe me that she's a tramp?"

"So much for all the promises of privacy." Their father looked as if he had received a crushing blow.

"Oh, God, Daniel, it's not the end of the world," said Harold.

"Well, is there a baby?" asked Dusty. "If there is, I'd love to see it. Is it a boy or a girl?"

"It's a little girl," Daniel said. "Her name is Jean Marie. We called her after our mothers, you see. Hoping they'd come around. But some hope that was."

"How old is she?" Dusty asked.

"Two and a bit," Daniel said.

"Can I see her?" Dusty's face was shining.

"I don't see why not. I see her every Saturday. You could come along with me," Daniel said.

Then there was another silence. But the world didn't come to an end or anything. So they went on with their meal. Where nobody talked much, as usual. After supper, Daniel went into the sitting room with Father. Dusty listened at the door.

"You promised that you wouldn't involve everyone else in this disgrace," her father said.

"I didn't and Molly didn't . . . . but since half of Dusty's school knows already—"

"And how do they know, might I ask?"

"Molly and I didn't tell anyone. Nobody knows she's my child. That's what we agreed. I go down on Saturdays and work in her father's shop for the whole day for wages, and I get to see the baby for an hour. That's my contribution to her life. Until I earn money. You don't pay anything. You don't lose anything, so why should I not take my little sister to see a baby who's her niece?"

"Do as you will. You always have." Dusty heard her father sigh a deep, heavy sigh.

On the way to see the baby, Dusty asked cheerfully, "Does she live in a tent or a dustbin or anything?"

"Heavens, no! What made you think that?"

"Mother said she was a tramp or that her mother was."

"I remember." He was grim.

"And I thought they might all be tramps in funny hats, like Charlie Chaplin."

"No, it's not like that at all. You know she's only six years younger than you. If things had been different, you could have grown up together. She'd have been like a little sister."

"How do you mean?"

"Well, Molly and I thought we could live over the garage, and Molly could mind you, too, when Mother went out to work. It would have been great."

"And why was it not great?"

"Search me." Daniel looked very unhappy.

If Dusty had been asked what the best day of her childhood was, she would have said it was the day she met Jean Marie. She was like a big doll who waddled around holding out her arms to everyone.

When Jean Marie heard Dusty's name, she said, "Dussy," and went straight into her arms. Dusty had never cuddled anything living before.

They didn't have a cat or a dog at home. And her mother wasn't very strong on hugs. There had never been anything as lovely as this baby with the huge dark eyes and the little dress with rosebuds on it. She smelled of talcum powder and soap. And she had little brown boots that laced up.

"Can't you lend her to Daniel for a bit, so that we could play with her at home?" she asked the woman called Molly.

"I'd love to, Dusty," Molly said. "But that's something that can't be done."

Miss Howe at school used to say that there was no such word as "can't." Everyone could do everything if only they tried.

"Look, you're a grown-up girl, Dusty," said Molly. "I'll say it to you straight. Your mother doesn't like me. Not everyone likes everyone. But that's why I can't come to see you or lend Jean Marie to Daniel, which I'd love to do."

"That's because she thinks you're a tramp," Dusty said helpfully. "Maybe she didn't want a tramp coming because of all the old clothes and everything, but once she knows you're not, then it should be all right."

Molly's eyes met Daniel's. They looked at each other as if deciding whether to laugh or cry and fortunately they decided to laugh. They laughed until tears came down their faces.

Dusty didn't see what was causing everyone such delight. She laughed, too, and so did Jean Marie. And the toddler put her arms around Dusty's neck and said, "I love you."

All during tea Molly and Daniel talked and laughed and Jean Marie beat on the table with her spoon and sang. Imagine being in a house where people talked all the time at mealtimes. Of course, this wasn't a real house. Dusty realized that straightaway. This wasn't how people behaved in a real home.

On Monday she told everyone about the new niece she had found. Dusty's friend Kate was a bit interested, but the others all had younger sisters and brothers at home. They didn't think it was such great news.

Dusty told Miss Howe. Miss Howe was interested. "That's great for you, Dusty. You can have a little friend always and you can tell her things, stories, and how to make a daisy chain, and how to keep a scrapbook. She'll always love you and come to you when she needs things."

"But she can't come home. She's not allowed to come to our house," Dusty said.

"In a way that makes it a better friendship," Miss Howe said, looking on the bright side. "You see, if she were at home all the time or always coming to visit, you might get tired of her, like all the other girls here get tired of their little sisters. This way she'll be a treat to you and you'll be a treat to her."

Dusty never mentioned her visits there to Mother or Father, because she knew it would upset them. But they knew where she went on Saturdays.

Molly was very nice. Sometimes she let Dusty put on her makeup, and she said Dusty could bring Kate, too, and they could dress up in her clothes. It was much better than bringing Kate home, because Mother worried so much about the dirt. Daniel told Dusty secretly that he was going to marry Molly when he was twenty-one and she was twenty-one. Dusty thought that was a pity. She would be too young to be a bridesmaid, too old to be a little flower girl. She and Kate planned what she would wear. She thought she'd like a yellow taffeta skirt and a scarlet jacket.

But she never got to choose. By the time he was twenty-one, everything had changed. Daniel was offered a travel scholarship to America. It would mean two years' study and visiting universities. It was too good an opportunity to pass up.

Molly would understand. And Jean Marie would understand. · After all, there had been long periods apart already. This time, when Dusty took Jean Marie by the hand for a walk in the park, they saw Molly crying on a park bench and Daniel standing up with his hands in his pockets, saying the same thing over and over.

"I'm not running away from you and the baby. Can't you see it's for the best?"

"What is it?" Jean Marie looked up trustingly at Dusty.

"I don't know, to tell you the truth, but I'll tell you when I do," Dusty said.

If anyone were to ask her how she became so successful in business deals, she would say, "I always tell people the truth, no matter whether it's good news or bad." She did that for the first time with the chubby toddler, who looked into her face for an answer. She promised that she would say what she found out. And she delivered on her promise.

Dusty found out that Daniel didn't want to marry Molly. That since he had been to college, he no longer loved Molly. All the things his parents had said would happen. So he had searched high and low for this travel scholarship that would take him away. Far away. He said he would write postcards to Jean Marie, but it would probably be best if he and Molly considered themselves free agents.

Molly cried a lot when she heard this. "I don't want to be a free agent," she said.

Dusty discussed it with Kate. There were two kinds of agents they knew about. Ones like Kate's mother were agents for some kind of mail-order firm. You ordered things and they came to Kate's house and her mother got a commission on what she sold. And then there were agents in spy films, like James Bond.

Molly seemed an unlikely person whom anyone would force to become either kind.

"Can I go on being friendly with my niece when you've gone away?" Dusty asked.

"I'd love it if you would, and maybe you might take pictures of her and send them to me," Daniel said. He had a very sad face.

"I'll take one every year on her birthday," Dusty said earnestly.

"Oh, well, that will be only two birthdays. That's not going to be much photography," Daniel said.

But Dusty knew somehow that he wouldn't be coming back.

So when Jean Marie was four she took the first one, and then when she was five.

And by the time she was six Molly said to her, "Don't bother, Dusty. He only throws them in the bin."

But Dusty went on and on. Jean Marie was seven and wore a new red dress bought for her by Molly's boyfriend, Ken, and then when she was eight she wore her flower girl's dress, the one she had worn at her mother's wedding. And when she was nine it was dungarees, and when she was ten it was jeans, and when she was eleven it was jeans again.

Dusty was seventeen now, of course, and very grown-up. She wrote to her brother Daniel only once a year. Once or twice he phoned home to ask her to write more often. He loved her long accounts of the life he'd left behind.

"You should be a writer, Dusty," he said. "You have a great gift of making me see the world very clearly. When I was your age, I didn't know what was going on around me."

"When you were my age you and Molly conceived Jean Marie."

"Well . . . I suppose that's one way of putting it. What a thing to say!"

"I was just saying it to assure you that you did know what was going on around you when you were seventeen," Dusty said.

"I wish you wrote more often," he said again.

"You never write to me at all. It's not easy to write to someone who doesn't write back. And you don't send Jean Marie post-cards. That's why she doesn't make you cards anymore."

"That sounds very calculating."

"No, it's not. It's about life being a bargain, isn't it? You give some things and other people give some things. That's how the world works, isn't it? I mean, you're out there in America in the heart of all that."

"Is that boy made of money that he can talk for hours and hours across the Atlantic?" Dusty's father asked when he walked into the room.

Father was fifty-seven now and a little bit testy. He had only two years and seven months before he retired from the office. The retirement was spoken of a lot. And whether there would be part-time work, relief work, consultant's work. It all seemed highly unlikely to Dusty, but her opinion was not asked, so she never gave it.

Mother was fussy, too, fussier than she used to be. The house was immaculate. Dusty got into the habit of leaving slippers just inside the door and putting them on the moment she came in.

She didn't bring friends home from school. Instead she brought them to Molly's. Molly and Ken were very easygoing; they were happy to see Dusty and her pals anytime, they said. And Jean Marie would make a great fuss over them.

"She's much nicer than the awful younger sisters people have," Kate said approvingly.

"Miss Howe was so right when she said that we like people much better if we don't live with them," Dusty said.

If Miss Howe was right, did it mean that you should leave home shortly after you were born in order to get on well with your family? It was a puzzle.

Jean Marie loved the way Dusty talked to her as if she were an equal.

"Do you think my father loves me much, much more because he's so far away?"

Dusty was honest, as always. "I'd say when he thinks of you, he loves you to bits," she said. "But he doesn't think of you *all* the time because he has to work and drive big long distances from one place to another."

Jean Marie nodded. It made sense.

"And if he were here living with Mum, would it be a different kind of love?"

"Yes, totally different—better in a way, because he'd be here all the time and you'd know him and he'd know you. But worse because it might mean that he and your mum weren't getting on well and that would be upsetting. And, of course, there'd be no Ken, and that would be awful, wouldn't it?"

They all loved Ken. That clinched it. Jean Marie was perfectly happy about it all and went off to make biscuits for them.

When Dusty left school, she told her parents her plans. "I'm going to do a very good, detailed course in office skills, word processing, office management, and, at the same time, I'm going to do a modeling course to give me confidence," she said.

They were horrified.

"But look at the university places you were offered," her father said.

"I've told everyone you were going to university," said her mother.

Dusty was calm. "I've just postponed it, that's all. I want to go to university when I know something about the world, not just rush in there when I'm silly and immature." She didn't say it, because it didn't need to be said, but there was her brother Daniel, almost a remittance man out in America, unable to face up to any responsibilities. Unsure, moving from place to place, always saying this one was for keeps and then moving again.

There was her brother Harold, who had failed out of one university and had received a mediocre pass degree from another. Harold was meant to be "in publishing." That was what their father said at the office, but, in fact, Harold was between jobs. He couldn't decide whether to marry his girlfriend or not, and she had left him. Harold lived sometimes at home and sometimes in a place he rented. In Dusty's view it wasn't much to have achieved at the age of twenty-eight.

"And how will you support yourself while you take these courses?" Mother wanted to know.

"I'm going to live with Molly and Ken and mind Jean Marie for them, so that's my bed and board, and I'm going to work in the café for Lionel's mum—that's my fees and clothes."

They were aghast.

"But why won't you live here? This is your home," they said.

She looked at them, old before their years, frightened people. Her father feared what they would think at the office when he told them of the humble aspirations his only daughter held. As if anyone in the office could care in the slightest. Her mother feared a change in the way things were, unable to see that the way things were was cold in an empty, loveless home, a place where people cared more about putting a coaster on the table for fear of causing a ring than how everyone else was getting on with their lives. She felt very sorry for them, even though she was only eighteen.

She knew that her own life might not turn out to be great and warm and all-embracing, but she was going to have a go at it. She wasn't going to resign herself to this kind of doomed caring about what other people might think . . . when she very deeply believed that most people were not thinking about you at all. And she also knew that at this particular point in her life, she would never abandon or ignore her parents the way her brothers had. She would make them glad that they had this late child who would love them much better from afar.

Dusty emptied her bedroom very carefully. She repapered it and lined all the drawers with scented paper. Then she chose some of her mother's best bed linens and made it up, ready to receive a guest. They could rent out the room.

"Perhaps someone working locally?" she suggested.

"A stranger in the house." Mother would hear nothing of it.

"You could give her a television and tea-making equipment in the room; then you wouldn't be falling over one another."

Father wondered what they would say in the office if they knew he was taking in paying guests.

"They wouldn't have to know unless you told them," Dusty said mildly. Her father agreed, surprised at the simplicity of it all.

"But where will you sleep when you come back to see us, Dusty?" her mother asked despondently.

"In one of the boys' rooms. We won't all be back at the same time, and if we are, someone can sleep on the sofa." Dusty made it all sound exciting, a full house, everyone home together. Something that would never happen. She helped her mother find a very pleasant lodger, a quiet woman who had come to work in a local lawyer's office.

"What a lovely house! I'm surprised you don't have more than one lodger," Miss King said.

So Dusty took the hint and helped her mother do up Daniel's room. He would never be back. Not for any length of time.

They found a Mr. Morris, and soon a common interest in cards was discovered.

Dusty wrote to her brothers. Daniel was in Pittsburgh and Harold had moved to Canada. She wrote and told them how happily Mother and Father were settling down with Mr. Morris and Miss King. She wrote to say how she had moved in with little Jean Marie, who was now twelve and very beautiful, and how she was back in the café where she had slept as a baby. And she was taking courses.

She felt that they didn't care very much. They sort of assumed that their mother and father would survive fine. Harold couldn't care less about Jean Marie. Daniel felt guilty about her. Neither of them knew or recalled that Dusty had slept as a baby between Lionel and Sergio in a café. But Dusty didn't mind. She was going to keep them informed of the situation at home as long as she lived. She was never going to lay any guilty feelings on them, making them feel they should be more involved. Just remind them of birthdays and tell them of various life events along the way.

So she wrote about Molly and Ken and how they ran a market stall together and were doing very well, and how bright Jean Marie had turned out to be, and how she did her homework every night in the café with Dusty to keep an eye on her. Sergio married a wild Italian girl who was very unfaithful to him, and Lionel had developed a wonderful little potbelly. She wrote about Mother and Father, who had been to a bridge weekend with Mr. Morris and Miss King, and how Father wasn't dreading his retirement from the office anymore.

She did not write and tell them how Lionel had fallen in love with her and was not to be consoled when she told him that the love was not returned. She did tell them that she didn't work at the café anymore. She did write when she finished school and discussed her future job. She didn't write about how much she loved the whole business of office routine, because it sounded somehow a bit pathetic.

She did tell them all about her move from one firm to another and a little bit about her rapid progress in every job she had. And she did tell them all about little Jean Marie getting accepted by the ballet school. She did tell them that Father was coping with retirement magnificently and couldn't understand how he'd ever found the time to work. She did not tell her brothers that this was almost entirely her own doing. From afar she organized her parents' lives very well.

She did not tell them that she had fallen in love with a man at work. A man not only married, but married to the boss's daughter. It was the ultimate cliché. If she had been writing a book on how not to organize your life, that was what she might have suggested. But it didn't feel like that, of course, when she had met Simon. It felt as if they had been meant for each other.

Dusty met Simon on her twenty-first birthday. He was twenty-five. As she was getting dressed to go to a party at a friend's, Jean Marie had asked whether she believed in love at first sight.

"Impossible," Dusty had explained. "It could only be attraction or infatuation or desire. Not love."

But that night Dusty fell in love with Simon—about five minutes after they met. It had something to do with his smile and the way he touched her on the arm and seemed at ease with himself. He wasn't fearful of a hug or a clasp or engaging with anyone, like her father was, like her brothers had been. Dusty often wondered how Daniel had ever coupled sufficiently with Molly in order to conceive Jean Marie. Simon was a warm, loving person. He reached out to be loved, and Dusty loved him from that very first night.

When people asked Dusty, as they often did, what the influences were that made her such a successful businesswoman, she said that it was a matter of luck and being able to grasp the chances as they came. She never felt any need to elaborate that her own luck had involved meeting Simon so early in her career and joining her future to his forevermore.

Simon thought Dusty was enchanting. That was the word he used the first time they met. He said he was under her spell. He also told her that he was married, so that there would be no misunderstanding.

But Dusty went back to her tiny bedroom in Molly and Ken's flat and stayed awake all night thinking about him. He was everything she had ever dreamed of or thought about in a man. Simon was like a great, bright star. She lay with her hands behind her head, wide awake, thinking how lucky she was to have met him. She never thought for one moment that it was a tragedy, a pity, or even a nuisance that he was married. She hadn't gone that far down the road of loving him. She just knew he was going to be the most important person in her life from now on.

"You don't need minding anymore," she said to Jean Marie, next morning at breakfast. "You're off to ballet school. I think I'll get my own place."

"Will you always be there for me?" Jean Marie asked. "I know it's very selfish, but I never minded my father not taking any notice of me, because you did."

"I'll get a flat with a spare room for you to come and stay as often as you like," she said.

And true to her word, she had found a place within a week. Lionel knew a good carpenter who worked nights, so Dusty got shelves and cupboards made. She had a kitchen created entirely to her own design and painted in warm colors.

Her mother and father's house was crowded with knick-knacks. She went back to find out if she could take some of the things that her mother had always described as clutter.

"Well, I don't know," her mother said.

"I mean, you'll get them when we're dead and gone," her father said.

Dusty had wanted to cry.

Lionel, in the café, gave her a gleaming new coffee machine, some colored saucepans, and cutlery with scarlet handles. Molly and Ken gave her a bright patchwork quilt. Sergio gave her Italian plates for the wall and for the table. Jean Marie planted window boxes for her. Her friend Kate helped her to make curtains. And then she felt she was able to invite Simon to visit her.

They had met many times at work. Simon was in the marketing division of the big mail-order firm that his father-in-law had started. It sold everything you could ever want. Dusty was in charge of customer services. When she felt that her new home was worthy to receive Simon, Dusty went to his office.

"I wanted to talk to you about a new scheme I have that might combine market research with customer services," she said.

"Sit down and tell me about it." His face was full of admiration for her, and more. Simon found that he genuinely liked Dusty.

"It is quite detailed," she said.

"Should we meet after work then, to give it the attention it deserves?" he wondered.

"That would be best, I think." Her heart was pounding.

He suggested a wine bar.

Too crowded and noisy, she said.

"And not enough space," he agreed.

"I don't live far away from here." She was tentative.

"That would give us space and time," he said.

She took her documents home, and a bottle of wine, and she lit a little fire, even though it wasn't a cold day. She didn't prepare a meal, because that might look too eager. But she had eggs and a great bowl of fresh vegetables in her kitchen. She could make an omelet if he stayed late enough. He stayed late enough. He loved the place.

"It's just the way I thought you'd live when I first met you," he said.

They sat at her little dining table, bought with this in mind, bought by Dusty only for Simon and herself . . . to sit at, work at, talk at . . . and then to leave when the time came to go into the bedroom with the glorious patchwork quilt.

When it all happened according to her hopes, it was as natural as could be.

"I love you," Simon said.

"Not as quickly as this, surely?" Dusty scarcely dared to hope.

"When you know, you know." Simon kissed her again and again.

Dusty's business plan had been a good one. She had invited subscriber customers to fill in a questionnaire about themselves, favorite colors, number of children, average spending power, hobbies. This went into the computer, first to build up a customer profile, but also as additional information beside each person's name and address.

"I know it sounds corny," Dusty said. "But I think if I were buying from a mail-order firm and someone in there remembered that I had a small apartment, no garden but three window boxes, a kitchen in gold and amber colors, and that I liked to listen to traditional jazz, I'd be pleased. It would be more personal than getting a lot of unsolicited advertisements for driving gloves or wheelbarrows. It would make me feel a bit special."

Together they worked on this. He got most of the credit, but that didn't matter, because Dusty got what she wanted, which was to have Simon at her side so much of the time, days and a lot of the evenings, too.

She asked no questions about his marriage. From the outset she had told him that he could look after that part of his life, and she never pleaded to see him on Sundays or at Christmas or at the times a married man might be expected to be in the marital home. She tried not to think about it too much.

She worked long hours and got a deserved promotion. She gave huge support to Jean Marie, turning up for every function at the ballet school and helping her save for a holiday abroad. She went back to working weekends in the café when they were busy and needed her. She found a cleaning woman for her mother, a window cleaner who came around four times a year. A grocer that delivered, to save her parents from standing for ages in long lines at the supermarket. And now they played bridge almost all afternoon and every night.

She didn't tell her mother and father about Simon because they never asked anything at all about her private life. They came once to see her flat and pronounced it very nice. Her mother said, of course, that it must be costing a fortune, and many a girl would be happy to live at home. It was a mild reproach for Dusty's having been bold enough to change things in a world like theirs, which resisted change even though it had improved their lives immeasurably.

And Dusty didn't know where the years went. Once a journalist asked her for milestones in her career. But she literally couldn't find any. She just worked longer hours, and was an even more devoted daughter than ever to her parents. She did their Christmas card lists; she organized social gatherings among their neighbors, sherry parties on the first Sunday of each month so that they would not become desert-island people with Miss King and Mr. Morris.

She stood proudly at the graduation ceremonies in Jean Marie's ballet school. She wrote regularly to her brothers and told them about the life they had left behind them with such little regret. Harold had since gone to a place in Australia, so Dusty used e-mail to write. She was tempted to do one e-mail for both her brothers and just insert a separate paragraph in each to make it personal. But somehow it didn't seem quite fair.

She had made a huge success of the mail-order firm and had built up the personal side of it, so that many customers used them almost as an agony aunt. They wrote about dinner dances coming up that were causing them anxiety. Dusty had arranged that each client was assigned to a personal adviser. These girls wrote sympathetic, encouraging letters suggesting, but never forcing, merchandise, counseling getting a dress slightly larger than one needed, and often advising dyeing shoes to match or getting their jewelry in a charity shop. Their clients felt these advisers were personal friends, and they were never tempted away by any other mail-order company whatsoever.

"I think I may be spoiling your life," Simon said to her many times. "Without me you'd find someone else, have a real life, children, a home."

"Without you I'd have no life," Dusty said. "I have a home, and Jean Marie is better than a child to me. I've missed out on nothing."

And so she believed. Shortly after her twenty-seventh birthday, she was made a senior partner, and then she was called into the office by the chief executive. He wanted a word, a confidential word. Dusty went in with an easy conscience. This man could be nothing but pleased with her. She had been responsible for huge profits, a high media image, and enormous customer satisfaction. Her discretion with his son-in-law had been absolute. They never appeared in public together.

Dusty went in, dressed as always in the smarter merchandise that the company sold. It looked well on her, because she had expensive Italian shoes, a real leather belt, and good jewelry. But it had been a stroke of genius to dress from the catalogs since she arrived. The photographers and journalists loved it, too.

"I can rely on you utterly," Simon's father-in-law said.

"Utterly," she said truthfully.

"I'm going to sack Simon. He's not trustworthy, Dusty," said the man who had first founded this company.

"Oh, I'm sure that's not . . . that's not the case." Her voice sounded strange in her own ears.

"I'm afraid it's true. He has been unfaithful to my daughter,

and if he cannot be honorable in the home, it is extremely unlikely he can be so in the workplace."

"Unfaithful?" Dusty waited.

Why had they made her a partner the previous week if they
were going to drag her down now?

"Yes, and with an arrogance that is staggering. He took this
girl to a trade fair in one of the major hotels in front of everyone."

Dusty felt nausea rise in her throat. Simon had another girl.

"But he said he went with his wife to the trade fair," she said.

She remembered it well. She had wanted to go. She had
every right to go, but Simon had insisted it was one of the few oc-
casions when he would have to be accompanied by his wife.

"Was it someone he's having a regular relationship with?"
Dusty asked.

"Yes, it's been going on for about two years, apparently.
They've been seen in restaurants and at discos and theaters. I
did hear rumors, but I decided not to believe them. I was
wrong." He looked like an old, sad man.

"And your daughter . . . ?"

"She's heartbroken. She doesn't want him sacked, but I will
not work with him. I tell you that."

"For two years," Dusty said wonderingly.

For two whole years, Simon had been rushing away from her
flat not to go home to his demanding and petulant wife, the
spoiled daughter of the boss, but to another girl. A girl he took to
dinners and discos and theaters.

"Yes, well, it's all over now," the old man said. "He goes today."

Was there something in his voice? Some distant wish to be
talked out of this very harsh response? Could Dusty save Simon
by pleading his case? It was a position of extraordinary power.

"Two years," she said again.

"Or thereabouts," the affronted father-in-law said.

"I'm afraid it does mean that he is not trustworthy," Dusty

said—and ended Simon's career. She didn't care whether it ended his marriage or not. It was immaterial now. He had never loved her.

She changed the lock on her flat door that day. She sat inside alone, listening as he fumbled with the key trying to get in. She remained perfectly still as he called and begged to be allowed to explain. Eventually he went away. He tried to see her in the office, but she always had a meeting or was in a conference. She asked that his calls not be put through.

"I'm afraid he's trying to use me as a go-between, and I want to stay completely out of it," she explained.

And then Simon told his father-in-law that he had been having an affair with Dusty. He said it had been going on for years.

"Just so you know she is equally untrustworthy," he cried.

Dusty had been there when the accusation was made. She just shook her head sadly.

"You know this is not so, Simon," she said.

The old man had looked slowly from one to the other. It was not hard to see which one was the fantasist trying to destroy everyone else in sight.

"I've had her key for years and years." He took the key she had given him on a heart-shaped key ring from his pocket.

"No, Simon," she said calmly, producing her own key.

Now a totally different shape, a different lock.

She left the room and she knew that there were now going to be injunctions served on Simon. He must not visit the premises again; he must desist from these threats. The very fact that their love affair had been so secret, so hidden, was a bonus now. No one had seen them together.

Her father telephoned that night.

"I've had some disturbing news about your mother," he said.

"Is she there? Can you talk?" Dusty asked.

"No, she's in the hospital, actually." He sounded bewildered.

"I'll come around," Dusty said.

Her father had been understating the disturbing news. It was very serious. Her mother had a tumor. They could not operate and there would be no treatment. They were talking about four months at the most.

"If I were still at the office I'd have some pattern to my days. I'd know better what to do," he said sadly.

She felt a surge of total irritation with him. What did it matter whether there was a pattern to his days or not? Her mother had such a limited span of days left. But she hid her irritation, as she so often had to at work. She said instead, "Would you like Miss King and Mr. Morris to continue living here, Father?"

"Yes, but I don't know what they would do about breakfasts and . . . things."

Dusty paused. One of her principles at work had always been that you should never rush in to volunteer anything unless you were perfectly sure you could do it.

She was sure.

"I'll come home for the winter," she said.

"And then later?"

"We'll think again then."

Being Father, of course, he couldn't say anything warm and generous. Tell her he loved her and thank her.

But Simon had been ready with the words, the assurances, and the smiles. Too ready and too generous. Maybe quick responses and fancy phrases were not the only currency that mattered.

"I'm coming home for the winter, Mother," Dusty said the next day in the hospital. Her mother wasn't really aware of the extent of her illness. "Why are you doing that?" she asked suspiciously.

"Well, for one thing, to keep an eye on you when you get out of the hospital, and for another I've had a romance that is over, and I'm feeling a bit lonely in the flat at the moment."

"I always thought it was foolish of you to go and live in that place," her mother said.

She arranged to give her flat to Jean Marie for six months.

"A flat of my own. Oh, Dusty, you're so good, you're so good. Can I do anything to thank you?"

"Yes. I'm spending the winter with my parents. If you could bear it, I'd like you to come and see them sometime."

"I thought they didn't want me."

"They don't know what they want," Dusty said with a laugh.

"I suppose you'll not work here anymore now that you're promoted," Lionel said in the café.

"I don't know why you say that."

"Well, you won't need the money." Lionel was defensive. He knew Dusty had done so well.

Sergio called in from the kitchen, "She never needed the money anyway, you great loon; she only comes because she loves us."

"Quite right," Dusty said briskly.

Mother came home and was pleased that nothing much had changed. Miss King and Mr. Morris were still part of the household, and nowadays everyone got their own breakfast from a plentiful supply of things in the kitchen. The café where Mother had worked so long ago provided fresh rolls every day: they were dropped on the doorstep by Sergio on his way home from work. Dusty had painted Harold's old room and was living there happily, as if she had never moved out to the apartment.

If Mother remembered Dusty's saying a romance was over, she never referred to it again.

They played a lot of bridge at night, and Dusty and Mother played together in case Mother was tired or forgot what trumps were. But Dusty said it was because she wasn't experienced herself.

And Jean Marie came two or three times a week. Nobody called anyone Grandfather or Grandmother. No reference was made to Daniel in America. Or to Molly and Ken. She was just a

friend, a young dancer. Everyone liked her and she made sandwiches and served them on bridge evenings.

At Christmas they invited Lionel, because he was on his own.
He helped Dusty to cook the turkey. Miss King and Mr. Morris
said they had never enjoyed a Christmas more. Jean Marie was
there as well, because Molly and Ken had gone to an alternative
health seminar in the north somewhere. After dinner, Daniel
and Harold rang from America.

When Daniel was on the phone, Dusty asked him to have a
word with Jean Marie.

"You sound so American," Jean Marie said to him in wonder.

"You sound so grown-up," he said in surprise.

"Will you send me a picture of yourself?" she asked.

"Yes. I'll get a haircut. Buy a new jacket, hold my gut in, and
have one taken," he said.

"I'm sure you look fine," Jean Marie said.

Dusty took the phone. A little emotion at a time was her rule
these days.

Mother got weaker in January. She didn't get up anymore.

Dusty arranged that her mother sleep downstairs in the dining room, which they rarely used. Lionel came and helped her to
make it more suitable. He called in most days on his way home
from the café. She looked forward to his visits and invited him
for dinner more than once.

He told her Sergio was getting married again in the spring.
He told her that he still had a picture of them all in prams, in the
old days. He also told her his plans for the café when his father
would retire next year.

Dusty's father never cried. He just went on being methodical
as always.

"I'm glad you came back for the winter," he said.

Dusty's heart beat faster. Father never said anything warm.

"I'm glad, too," she said.

"It gives a pattern to my days, somehow," he said.

"You loved the office, didn't you?" Dusty said.

"No, I was afraid of it, in fact . . . but you knew where you were there, even in a lowly sort of way. You knew what was expected. I never quite knew that anywhere else," he said.

There was a pause.

"Don't get too fond of your office, Dusty," he said.

"No, Father," she said in a small, quiet voice.

She told Daniel to pretend that he had business in England.

"Do come over and see Mother," she said.

"But won't that alarm her? I was going to come for the funeral."

"No, come while she's here," Dusty said. And she called the travel agent to get a ticket for him.

Dusty made sure that he met with Jean Marie. She didn't leave them alone for too long.

"I'm sorry I was so out of touch," he said, holding his twenty-one-year-old daughter in a bear hug.

"You were never really out of touch. Dusty told me everything I ever asked," she said.

After she sent four frantic e-mails to Harold, he showed up, looking scruffy and unkempt. Dusty borrowed a shirt, jacket, and tie from Lionel.

"Just that Mother might think a bit better of him," she apologized.

"You don't have to say," Lionel said, and gave his good gray flannel trousers as well. Harold had only jeans.

The night before her mother died, Dusty sat by the bed.

"You have no pain?" Dusty asked.

"None at all. These modern drugs are good. I think things get better really, not worse, like other people say."

"Oh, I'm sure you're quite right," said Dusty.

"Will you marry Lionel?" Mother asked.

"What?"

"You heard me."

"I heard you, but I can't believe you asked."

"He will ask when I've gone. You're normally prepared for things, always so organized and everything."

"I'm not really." Dusty's eyes were full of tears; the casual way her mother referred to being gone was heartbreaking. But also calming in a strange sort of way.

"Do you like him?"

"Yes, of course, I like him, but . . ."

"But you think there's something else, something more exciting."

"I've had that." Dusty was grim.

"Good. Then you're probably ready for Lionel."

She fell asleep then.

The next day, she thanked Dusty—in a brisk, matter-of-fact way, as if she were saying thank you to a friend for paying the bill in a tea shop.

And then she died—very quietly and without anxiety or any struggle.

The first crocuses were coming up when Lionel asked her to marry him.

He brought the picture of them all in their prams with him to help him make the proposal.

"I know I'm not very exciting . . ." he began.

"Yes, I'd love to," Dusty said.

"What? You don't know what I'm going to say," he said.

"I do, and I'd love to," she said.

He held her in his arms.

"I've always wanted to, and when you came home here for the winter, I thought . . . 'Well, Dusty might need me for this hard winter, when everything's so sad, but then she won't want me anymore. She'll want to put the memory of the sad winter behind her and go off and live her life.' "

She was glad she had come home for the winter.

Suppose Simon had still been with her and with his wife and

with another woman . . . none of this would ever have happened. She would not have gotten to know her mother, understood her father. And best of all, find the boy in the pram next door.

"When will we get married?" He could hardly believe it.

"As soon as we can," she said.

It had been one of her great strengths, they said in the office, that when she made her mind up she did something straightaway.

She would work fewer hours in the office from now on. She would spend more time in the café.

"We'll tell Sergio to hurry up and have a baby, so that we can set the prams up again in the yard," she said.

If something was worth doing, it was worth doing well.

Think of the story as a journey. Something happens to the main character at the start, and we follow him or her dealing with it, or not dealing with it, or ignoring it, or making it worse.

—Maeve Binchy

A Week's Work

When Maire asked to leave the resort and go back home to Dublin for her grandfather's funeral, the travel company said yes, just as long as she picked someone else to mind the tourists. It wouldn't be too much of a job, just someone to be in charge, to take complaints, to book excursions, to keep an eye on things. Mainly everyone just went to the beach all day and to the bars and cafés all night; they found their own fun. Get some reliable girl from the guests, Maire was told, offer her a week's work, a free holiday, and a few quid. Then she could take the time off.

Maire looked at the guests thoughtfully for a while. It was hard to know whom to choose. This job wasn't quite as easy as everyone thought, not just a matter of lounging around in the sun all day. There were always things to do, not to mention the emergencies. Maire would need to get someone levelheaded.

She wondered whom she would find to offer the week's work. The reliable ones had jobs of their own and wouldn't be able to drop them suddenly to spend an extra week in the resort. There was one woman; she wasn't like the others. She was quiet; she read a lot by the pool; she walked alone along the beach with a big, shady hat. She didn't join in much, but you couldn't say either that she was standoffish, and she would always have one drink at the sangria parties that the various restaurants organized every evening, hoping to attract customers for the night.

Her name was Sara; she said she was a freelancer. But she never said a freelancer of what. On an instinct, Maire trusted her. She explained the job carefully, the most important item being in a week's time, when Sara would have to collect all the clients from the different hotels in a bus and deliver them safely onto the plane. The difficulty of that particular transport was increased by the fact that the plane left late, and they would have had the whole day in the sun to get burned to a crisp and sample as much sangria as they could swallow before boarding the plane.

Although she herself wasn't a foolish sunbather, nor an unwise drinker, Sara seemed to understand this problem. She was calm and appeared to see no difficulties. Maire, feeling that she had made a wise choice, went out to the airport and back to Dublin for the funeral. On the plane home Maire remembered that she hadn't asked Sara what she did for a living. Perhaps she should have.

But then she thought that was being too fussy; you had to go by gut feeling. Sara would be able to cope with all that being a courier would throw at her. Wouldn't she? Perhaps Maire could telephone Pablo the driver to make sure there were no real dramas. Silly-mother-hen-like, of course, but she would do it, just for her own peace of mind.

Day One: Pablo told her that one of their tourists had danced on a tabletop too near a ceiling fan and sliced open his head. Maire sat down, feeling very faint, but apparently Sara had decided he needed stitches and driven him to a hospital herself. Sara had said there was no need to contact the company.

Day Two: Pablo reported that eleven of their fifty-eight clients had food poisoning. Sara had found a doctor, given them all boiled water, and encouraged the faulty and weeping restaurant owner to give everyone free dinners for a week. No need to contact the company.

Day Three: Pablo said there was a real drama. The tour company had phoned to say that a lady's husband had died in Ireland. The lady couldn't be found because she had gone off on a motorbike for three days with a local romeo.

Weakly, Maire wondered what Sara had done. She had rented a motorbike and gone after them, apparently.

Day Four: It turned out that Sara had found them and sent the grieving widow home on someone else's charter flight.

Day Five: Sara had held a prayer ceremony by the pool for the lady's deceased husband and got a picture of the proceedings taken, which would, Sara said, be a great consolation to the bereaved family later.

Day Six: Sara had stopped an international brawl by walking into the middle of it all and saying that she was very sorry she had to take the Irish tourists back to the hotel now, this minute, in a bus, because there was Huge, Momentous News from Ireland she had to break to them. The news was that she realized that they were outnumbered, and would undoubtedly lose. This way she had saved face for them.

Day Seven: Pablo said that the bus had left on time, with everyone on board and sober, heading for the airport, where they were going to play charades in the departure lounge, and there would be prizes of Spanish brandy for the best performances, the prizes to be handed over by Sara at the Dublin airport once they had disembarked.

Maire was worried. True, she had wanted someone reliable, but not a genius, not someone who would take over her job. After all, Sara had said she worked freelance. Maire decided that she would go to the airport and meet the returning clients and—the real purpose of the visit—sort this Sara out once and for all.

The clients all came in like lambs, sober lambs. Each of them got a wrapped bottle of brandy, gifts, apparently, from grateful restaurant owners, who regarded Sara as some kind of saint and had begged her to stay on for the season. Or so the clients told Maire.

"And did you feel you might like to?" Maire said, through gritted teeth and narrowed eyes when she finally met Sara.

"Oh, I might have, but not now. I have a lot of work to do here. I've got to start tomorrow."

"What exactly *do* you do?" Maire asked.

"This week it will be an inner-city playground, next week a rehab center." Sara spoke casually.

"You're a social worker?" Maire gaped.

"No, I'm actually a nun," Sara said.

"Nuns aren't freelancers," Maire said.

"They often are these days. You sort of turn your hand to anything. I was actually thinking we should ask some of the younger sisters to try a spell as a holiday courier," said Sara cheerfully. "They'd see a fair bit of life and get an idea about human nature. You *are* courageous, Maire. I'll pray for you."

And she was gone, to take the bus into Dublin and get on with her life.

Twelve Columns

Written for the *Irish Times*

THE FALL.

⌒

Years ago, before I knew that people called things by different names, we knew an American person named Martha and she used to talk a lot about the fall. I didn't know it was autumn for ages, because she had so many other marvelous expressions and dramas in her life that the thought of a huge upcoming fall off a roof or a wall or something was only too likely. After all, her father had lost all his money in the Crash, and we thought it was a car crash and asked why he didn't go back to the scene where the crash had happened and look for it. And when she talked about little cookies we thought she meant small people in chefs' outfits.

I call her a person, not a girl or a woman, because we thought she was oldish, almost bordering on being an adult. She was the cousin of a neighbor and she came to spend four weeks' vacation every year. She used to clean the house from top to bottom as payment for her keep. She talked about Jell-O and turnpikes and trash cans, and how her uncle used to take the paddle to his sons if they behaved badly.

Mostly we didn't know what she was talking about, but she seemed to treat us as equals, which was great. It was a time when it was much more important that people were of goodwill and occasionally had candy to offer than that we understood what they were talking about. We were always pleased when Martha arrived, and we listened, bewildered, to some of the things she said.

Like, back home she worked for a tightwad who ran an old folks' home, and her brother hoped to hang out his shingle and her sister had saved for a muskrat coat. And always she said she wished she could stay in Ireland for the fall. She would love to see just one fall in this part of the world. It would be wonderful, what with there being so much greenery already.

I didn't ask anyone about it, because, to be honest, I got the impression that the grown-ups thought Martha was a bit soft in the head, and I didn't want to let her down, and I thought it was odd to look forward to and be wistful about seeing a fall of any sort. And I had no idea what greenery had to do with anything.

And the years went on and her uncle's wife died and he didn't see any need to drag the unfortunate Martha back to be a skivvy in the house. Those were his words. His late wife had always referred to it as giving the girl a holiday. But anyway, Martha didn't come. And sometimes she sent us the funnies from American newspapers—Blondie and Dagwood and things—and we got a lot of the jokes in them.

And one day some years later her uncle said that some people were just born for trouble, and that Martha had all the hallmarks of that kind of person. It wasn't bad enough that her father had lost all his money on some cracked stocks and shares; her brother had been forbidden to practice law because of some misunderstanding; her sister had left home without a forwarding address. Martha's mother was in decline, so they had arranged that the mother go into the home where Martha worked—no wages for Martha, but then no fees for the mother.

I was about fourteen then.

"It's not fair," I said.

Martha's uncle said that in his opinion life was rarely fair.

Martha didn't remember what age we were, or else she thought we'd still like the funnies, and when I was about sixteen, I actually got her address and wrote to thank her. She wrote back to tell me she was in love.

And this was fantastic. First, nobody talked much about love, no one old, like in their twenties, which Martha was, and she told me that his name was James and his aunt was a patient in the home and that when his aunt died James would be very rich and they would get married. And I was very excited by this and asked what kind of things James said, and Martha rather innocently wrote and told me, and I told them to the girls at school.

And Martha said that when she and James got married they would come to Ireland for a honeymoon—they would come for the fall. I knew what the fall was now, but I didn't rate it much in those days. I wrote and told her that she shouldn't bother; the summer was nicer, and of course she wouldn't have to clean her dead aunt's house now. I even said that she had been very good to do all that years ago. And she wrote an odd letter saying that she looked back on those days like heaven; the work was so much easier than there in the old people's home. She would love to leave, but of course there was her mother to support there, and then James coming in twice a week to see his aunt.

I always thought she was a nurse there, but she was a lowly cleaner, she explained. She said that she had never claimed to be anything else. She asked for a picture of Ireland in the fall.

We didn't have color films in our cameras in 1956, and our garden looked desperate anyway, and my mother said why wouldn't I take a snap of it when there was something to see instead of everything straggling and dying. I found a wet-looking picture postcard that looked as if it were taken in famine times and sent it to Martha. She didn't reply and then we lost touch.

And when I was twenty and saw the colors of my first fall in New England, I remembered Martha and wrote to the old people's home that the tightwad had run. I didn't know his actual name, but a woman wrote back and said that Martha didn't work there anymore, adding that the management had entirely changed.

And I felt somehow that Martha had been annoyed with me for sending her that horrible postcard, so I wrote again and wondered did they know where she was, because I wanted to send her a proper picture of Ireland.

And the woman wrote to say Martha was in a penitentiary, she and a young man had been convicted of the killing of the young man's aunt. . . . It had always been thought that Martha was very much under the young man's influence.

Martha's mother had died shortly after it, her brother had been in some kind of trouble, and there was no trace of her sister.

Her uncle in Dublin is long dead.

Martha would be sixty-five now.

It's not her real name, but if she were out there and on the Internet? Maybe I would find her.

On this lovely autumn day when the fall in Ireland never looked better, I would love to find her, and to take her back to see it just once. I don't want to hear about James; I don't imagine she sees much of him.

There are greater coincidences in the world than that I should find her and show her the Irish autumn she wanted so much to see.

MY THEODORA STORY

Last week, when I was writing about sauces in a restaurant, I felt the familiar sense of fear that Theodora might read it and tell me that even now at this late stage I had still learned nothing about cookery terms.

But last Saturday the pages were full of appreciations and memories of Theodora FitzGibbon, and I remembered my own Theodora story and how she had said I must always tell it after she was dead, since it reflected huge credit on her and George and none at all on me.

I *think* I was the one who hired Theodora on a regular basis for the *Irish Times*. The more famous she became the more often I say that it was I who found her. Anyway, when I became women's editor in 1968, knowing nothing about fashion and cookery, it was great to have that side of things handled by experts. In the beginning she used to discuss recipes with me, but the feeling of talking to a brick wall must have overcome her, because she eventually gave up. One inkling of my limitations may have come when she typed out a recipe that included one to one and a half pounds of split peas. The way it was written, a 1 and then another 1 and a ½, made me think it must have been eleven and a half pounds that she meant, and I amended her copy accordingly.

It was around that time that she decided to take control of her own column, and sometimes her husband, George Morrison, would send us a picture to go with the piece that Theodora wrote. I loved it when he did, but it was always just a little bonus.

So there was this day when it came to getting the cookery page ready and it was one of the days that George hadn't sent an illustration. The recipes were for various ways of cooking veal. Of course, because I wasn't well organized there was no time to ask the *Irish Times* photography department to set up a nice relevant picture, so I looked through what I always called my Emergency Cookery Pictures File. These were things that had come from various sources, you know, pots of marmalade beside oranges, and picnic hampers. Nothing seemed very suitable until I saw a nice, vague-looking picture of a casserole with a lot of spoons and servers and forks sticking out of it. . . . It wasn't the *best* but it would do, I told myself. A swift caption was typed by me: "Tasty veal casserole, excellent for a winter evening," and with the totally undeserved feeling of a job well-done, I took the train out to Dalkey at the end of the day.

My father and I were looking at the nine-o'clock news on television when I saw something that made me deeply uneasy. I saw Dr. Christiaan Barnard, the heart transplant surgeon, getting off a plane somewhere after yet another successful operation, and I knew suddenly where I had seen that picture before. It was in fact a picture of openheart surgery. What I had taken to be forks and servers were in fact clamps and forceps.

I telephoned the paper and asked them to hold the cookery page. As a request at ten past nine at night, it was poorly received. I was asked why, and the explanation was met with disbelief.

"I think you had better get in here as quickly as possible," said the editor in a voice that I knew was holding on by only a thread.

We had no car, so I started to run the nine miles from Dalkey to Dublin purple-faced, panic-stricken. An unknown man with a car gave me a lift, and when he heard my errand he abandoned his car in the traffic in D'Olier Street and came in with me, a total stranger, saying he had to see; he loved to know how other people coped in a crisis.

Grimly, I discovered, very grimly. They stood around my desk searching hopelessly for any alternative picture; not having unearthed the Emergency Cookery Pictures File, they had found only a cache of Kit Kat wrappers and a bundle of magazines of a much lower brow than I would have liked it known I read.

The replacement picture had to be of the same size. There was now no time to enlarge or reduce anything that emerged from the file. Eventually I found one, an egg in an egg cup . . . I think it was a picture from an advertising agency trying to show the charms of some china.

Underneath the picture, and under the grim glance of Top People, I typed out: "Why be content with a boiled egg on a winter's evening when you could have all these tasty veal recipes?"

Theodora was on the phone bright and early.

"You didn't exactly kill yourself getting an illustration," she said to me frostily. But she was delighted with the explanation of the terrible happenings of the night before. She said she had lived a colorful life and it would have been entertaining to have added a prosecution for cannibalism to her other achievements. She seemed to regret my last minute discovery and heroic dash to save us all from turning out a cookery page that would have been a collector's item.

She said almost wistfully that it would have been something that would make people remember her . . . as if there were a chance that any of us will ever forget Theodora.

WISHING YOUR LIFE AWAY

There's a slightly irritating expression going around nowadays, when people say "I wish" or "You wish." Suppose someone tells you you're looking great, you must have lost weight, and you answer, "I wish," meaning, I suppose, you only wish that it were so.

Or else you say in a lovely, positive way that you're going to declutter your house and have lots of lovely empty creative space all around you, and someone says in a down-putting way, "You wish," meaning in your dreams you're going to do this.

I think it's because I never liked the whole concept of wishing for things that I dislike this expression. You see, what people usually wish for is something they either have or haven't power to get. If they have power to get it then they should try to have it, and if they don't, they should accept that.

When I was fourteen I wished I were smaller: not just thinner, but that I were actually five foot one inch and that people would pat me on the head and bring me to the front of things where I could see, instead of leaving me at the back because I could see over everyone.

And I used to read about people who were eight feet tall who had mighty operations to shorten their spines or their legs or whatever, and I wondered if I could get one. I saved three pounds toward one once, which was mighty saving in those days.

I told my mother that if I were small and had curly hair I'd be the happiest person in the world. She said she could get me curly hair, anyway, and on Saturday afternoon we went down to a hairdresser in Dun Laoghaire and, with a lot of torture, I had a fairly unwise perm.

But she said there was nothing any of us could do about being tall except possibly pull our shoulders back and enjoy it. Which, of course, I didn't do.

And then when I was seventeen I wished I had a duffel coat. That was possible—difficult, but possible. It meant living on half my pocket money for two terms, and taking sandwiches to town for lunch, but I got my wish.

When I was eighteen I wished that a fellow loved me like I loved him, but he didn't, and there were no witch doctors with magic potions, so instead I wished that the girl that he did appear to love would emigrate or fail her exams at UCD or both, but neither of those things happened either.

There was a lot of wishing that year, I remember. I was in France, very unhappy on an exchange visit, but pretending to my kind parents who had paid for it all that it was great. I wished fervently that Monsieur would stop pinching me black and blue, but he didn't stop. I also wished that Ballymoss would win the Arc de Triomphe Stakes at Longchamps, because for some reason—bad communication with my hopeless French or something—the whole family I was staying with seemed to think I had the inside track on this racing business and they were all putting everything they had on him. And Ballymoss *did* win, God bless his or her little flanks.

But my wishing did no good in either case; they were just things that happened. Monsieur would have pinched the flesh off anyone who came into that house, and Ballymoss didn't know that the fortunes of the whole of Compiègne and its environs were dependent on his or her winning that particular race.

And when I began teaching I used to wish that there would be no smart-aleck kids in the class who would know more than I did. But there was a solution to that: you had to prepare your lessons properly and get to know more than they did, so that wish could be granted.

There was no *point* in just wishing, like a lot of people did, that cigarettes were cheaper, that there were no school on Saturday mornings, that teachers were better paid, that there were more theaters in Dublin, that there wasn't so much poverty and inequality all around us. You could either try to change it or you shut up about it.

If I wasn't prepared to become a militant member of the Association of Secondary Teachers of Ireland, attend all the Easter conferences, and march with a placard, then the alternatives were to make do with what they paid us or work extra hours and get more.

If I truly cared about the unequal chance people got in life, then the answer was to *do* something, join a political party, stand for office, raise money for causes, help out on a practical level, or give it a rest and stop bellyaching about it.

Oh very stern, Maeve, someone said to me, when I said how much I hated all the wishing that's going on around me, very puritan, highly cut and dried. Why don't you allow people the indulgence of wanting the world to be a better place and their own lives to be marginally improved without insisting they rush out with a ten-point plan?

I suppose it's because people often think wishing is enough.

If they say over and over that the litter problem is out of hand and they wish so much that there were some proper recycling, they think they have somehow discharged their responsibility.

But they haven't, really; I think they have only added to the bleating.

In my stern book they would do much better to get a bottle bank or paper collection going, and organize communal trips to the dump.

Through community councils and parish groups' local newsletters they could campaign for less wrappings in supermarkets and shops, more litter bins in the streets, higher pay for road cleaners, and through the schools they could plead for more programs on awareness of such problems. If all the parents in a school demanded it, you can be quite sure the school would provide it.

One person concerned about litter is a well-meaning crank; two hundred of them means the job gets done. But just wishing the place were better means only joining the head-shaking, finger-wagging brigade who have changed nothing over the generations. I'd honestly prefer the people who just stepped over or walked around great mounds of litter, having decided that it's not their problem and therefore they are not going to mouth off useless platitudes about it.

What do you wish right now? Go on. Today, Saturday.

I bet you can divide your wishes into the things you can do some little thing about and those you can't. Better weather? No. But you could get wellies and a rain hat and go out all the same. To be thinner? Yes. You eat less. Win the lotto? No, but you could think that if you didn't buy the weekly ticket you would save £52 by this day next year. Find a life mate? Yes, you could stop wishing and go out to places where such a person might lurk, such as dating agencies, pubs, and the dog track. Change your spouse's way of going on? No. You have to change your own way of reacting to it or leave the spouse.

None of this is very new, nor indeed very puritan at all. It's all there in a prayer, apparently a grand prayer about wanting to accept what can't be changed, change what can, and the wisdom to know the difference between the two. Now once you've taken that on board then you'll stop all this endless, fruitless wishing. Won't you?

DUTCH COURAGE

They say that the easy way to find your way around Amsterdam is to remember that the canals go in order of ascending importance, first the Princes' Canal, then the Emperors', and then at the pinnacle the Herrengracht, the Gentlemen's or the Merchants' Canal. The Dutch way was always to rate the businessmen. If you remember that you won't get lost.

On the Herrengracht there is a beautiful, tranquil hotel called the Ambassade—it's so discreet that you would pass it and not know it was a hotel at all. Eight old Dutch houses, all with their own front doors—just one of them with a tiny foyer. From the bedroom window, you can see the canal flowing by, with closed-in boatloads of sightseers who point up at the lovely buildings, like the one you are sitting in.

There were people coming over to go to the Vermeer exhibition in The Hague—impossible to get a ticket for it now unless you booked with a group that includes entrance as part of the package.

There's a magnificent catalog that is selling in huge numbers. People were poring over it in the little space that acts as a lobby in the Hotel Ambassade and you could look out the windows and imagine that every single building opposite you housed a Vermeer scene inside.

One couple, disappointed not to get entrance tickets to the exhibition, were making the best of it. "We'll buy the catalog, dear, and tour around imagining *The Lacemaker*, *The Geographer* in any of these places," he said.

"And we can go to Delft, where he was from," the woman said eagerly, and they belted their raincoats and went off happily along the cobbled street.

At lunchtime a French author was being asked to sign two books for someone. "What will I write?" she asked, with a deeply puzzled expression. Would she write "Kind Wishes," or "Best Regards," or "Cordially"? Then, of course, it was for Dutch people—perhaps she should write something in Dutch? she asked. It was explained that they all spoke English, and would understand a word such as "Greetings." Greetings? No, she didn't think so. Not greetings. She opened her Dutch phrase book. It didn't yield her much. Very alarmist, all these things . . . Where is the ambulance? Where is the nearest hospital?

They watched glumly, the people who had been sent to get the signature. The author went through "left," "right," "double bed," "twin beds." "Oh, look," she said. "*Aardappels* . . . Imagine that's the Dutch for potatoes!" Then she found the word for Thursday—*Donderdag*. She said it over and over, and wondered if it would be a nice thing to write.

"Perhaps just 'Greetings' and your name?" they suggested desperately. They had forgotten how she hated "Greetings," a cold word, an almost hostile word.

They returned to the agonizing debate between "wishes" and "regards" when I had to leave. I was straining to see the title of her book, but couldn't. We have to hope it wasn't a tome on decision making. We have to weep for the people who went to her book signing and may still be there.

Roddy Doyle was heading off from the hotel for *his* book signing later that evening. The bookstore said he had attracted a great crowd, all of them anxious to talk to him about everything from teaching to holidays in Ireland, to the movies of his books. The shops are full of his books and he has a very big following.

Like everyone else, he doesn't know why the Dutch even consider translating anything written in English into their own language. Everyone you meet speaks such perfect English, they barely need the translation. But this would be a rude and ungracious thing to say to a Dutch publisher, and so nobody says it.

One of Roddy Doyle's admirers told me that his books were terrific; they really caught the way people spoke at school. Everyone in his school spoke exactly like that. Not the same words, obviously, because they spoke Dutch, but the same mood. It's the same all over the world, but nobody wrote it before.

One of my own outings was to a shopping mall in the far-distant suburbs, where I had some interesting encounters. Among the courteous, multilingual Dutch people who came to chat were two very bad-tempered women, indeed. The advertisement for the book signing had included the Dutch words for "a born storyteller." Apparently on the basis of this, they thought I had a new book out called *A Born Storyteller* and were very peeved that this was not so. They had read everything else; they had only come in, taking two buses, because they had been led to believe by a misleading newspaper ad that there was a new book.

I had no idea what all the shouting at the desk was about and kept looking up in alarm. When it was explained I offered them the bus fare, but they said it was the principle of the thing. They would go off and have a nice drinkey lunch instead. The bookseller thought that they might have already had a nice drinkey bus journey.

Then a man said he would like a book signed for his fiancée. "What's her name?" I asked, and he said something so extraordinarily unexpected to me that I nearly fell off my chair.

But it's amazing how you can recover, so I didn't even show my upset. I started to write my own name; and then he said it again. Now, this is very unreasonable I thought to myself. I didn't ask him to come in here and buy the book; he came of his own free will.

He looked at me despairingly. "Look, I'll write it out for you; her name, it's F-a-c-k-y-e."

"Of course it is," I said briskly, and sent her greetings, best wishes, and warm regards.

I flew from Schiphol Airport, an unmercifully huge place nicely serviced by little buggies, on a very small plane to Bristol. Beside me there was a man reading the *Daily Telegraph*. As always, everyone else's paper seems more interesting than the one you are reading, and when he had fallen asleep I took his paper from his nerveless hands and read it from cover to cover.

KLM had served a snack and told us proudly on a little note on each tray that they were introducing an experimental lobster snack, a small portion in a little dish; and it was only gorgeous. I was thinking to myself that it should be a fairly permanent experiment when I noticed that the sleeping man had eaten everything else on his tray but had not touched the lobster. I contemplated it, but decided reluctantly against it.

When he woke, I gave him back his newspaper. "I *was* thinking of eating your lobster as well," I said, hoping he would say: "But please do; I've always been allergic to it." Instead he went pale.

"My God, you can't shut your eyes for two minutes on a plane these days," he said. "I've been saving it, saving it as a treat." I don't think he was. I don't think he had intended to eat it at all, to be honest, it's just that he didn't like being unconscious while those around were making free with his newspaper and studying his snack tray.

I watched him at Bristol. He took out his mobile phone and told someone that he would check in at the hotel, unpack his dinner jacket, and freshen up before dinner. He was going to a big dressed-up dinner and he said he had been saving his lobster as a treat. A likely story.

IT WAS ONE OF THOSE
CUSTARD HEART DAYS

"In five weeks' time it will all be over," said the woman with the neatly zipped tartan shopping bag on wheels. She was full of triumph at having worked it out. "All over and done with," she said, in case any of us thought that Christmas might linger on a bit this year and trickle through until February. Her mouth was a thin line of satisfaction at having tamed the prospect of any festivity. She cast a gloom over everyone shopping in the late-night grocery.

It was one of my custard heart days. Sometimes I'm like a weasel with these killjoy people. But maybe she had a sad life. It could be that her husband had died during the year, or that her daughter had gotten married to someone they didn't like, and there had been a row.

Perhaps she had come from a home where they didn't ever celebrate Christmas much, or even something horrible could have happened at Christmastime and every year it came back to her. In one of my rare acts of kindness I smiled and said that it was true that there was a lot of fuss made about Christmas, all right.

The Lord punishes the insincere. I didn't mean it at all.

I was only saying it to please her. It was the wrong thing to do. I had misread her signs totally.

"Well, that's as may be." She sniffed at me disapprovingly. "And I'm the first to say live and let live. But I think it's a pity when folk can't have one short season of the year when they spread a little goodwill." She looked me up and down sadly.

"I daresay that you have your own reasons for hating Christmas, and I wouldn't presume to intrude and ask what they are. But perhaps I might say this: if you and the other people who hate Christmas were to think of the innocent little children who enjoy it, and the old people who have parties in the senior center, and comedians and personalities giving their free time to dress up as Santa Claus in hospitals, then you might think a bit more warmly about it."

Well, what would you have done? Tell her that you were lying in the first place, pretend to be converted to her bossy, cliché-ridden view of the world? Go deaf and wander off in the other direction? Abandon the wire shopping basket and run out of the late-night grocery? Wave at a mythical friend? Nod sagely with the all-purpose and meaningless cockney response: "Well, this is it. Isn't it?"

I was rescued. A man with the most bad-tempered face I have ever seen outside a cartoon came pounding into the late-night grocery. He headed straight for the woman with the unctuous views and the tartan shopper on wheels.

"May I just ask you one question? Just one? Did you come in here for a conversation session with total strangers, or was it possibly, as you claimed, for the shopping? I only ask because I have two traffic wardens up my arse outside, I've been around the block twice and we've missed ten minutes of *Sports Night* already."

I could see why she wanted a little goodwill in her life:

both of them working late, London traffic being like a medieval view of hell, crowds, queues, short tempers. I looked at what she had bought as it was being checked out and she packed it neatly into the shopping basket on wheels, which was totally unnecessary, since she had a husband and car outside the door. She had a lot of cat food, three kinds of cleaning stuff, and wire wool and big black plastic bags. She had one lamb chop, two apples, and a tube of indigestion tablets. It seemed a poor haul for someone whose mate was missing *Sports Night*, and I keep hoping that they do have a cat.

I have a friend who works in a bookshop and who is constantly amazed by the things people buy as Christmas presents. Men buy *Cooking for Idiots* and expect to get a tinkle of female laughter when the paper is ripped off it on the day.

Women buy *The Duffer's Golf Guide* . . . and expect a similarly delighted response.

My friend, who hasn't the same wish to enter into other people's lives as I do—and has certainly not the time sitting at a busy till in a large bookshop—says she arranges gift wrapping, or personalized red Christmas bags for books, without blinking an eye at the lack of wisdom involved in the choice. Until this week.

A nice young man, blond hair falling into his eyes, eager to a fault, hesitant and cursed with that overapologetic manner that some people wrongly think is politeness, approached her. He wanted to know about this service called Post-A-Book, which means that you pay the shop for the postage, address the envelope, and they'll send it off for you.

The book was addressed to a woman, and he signed a card with what was presumably his own name, since he paid with a credit card and it was the same name as on the card. "Merry Christmas, Darling. Love from Harry," he wrote, and put it in with the book.

The book was called *A Guide to Better Sex*, and the subheading said that it was a manual for those who found that the fizz had gone out of sex and who noticed that things were not as they used to be in the first heady days of their relationship.

Even the sight of a queue forming up behind the eager young man didn't stop my friend from making a last-ditch stand.

"It's a bit technical, this book, I believe," she began.

"Oh, yes, so it says," the young man said happily.

"I wonder, is it a suitable Christmas present? It's more a thing someone might buy for herself or himself, or sort of after a bit of chat, you know?" She was desperate now.

"No." He was firm. "No. I think she'd like it, and I'm sending it early because . . . well, she'll have plenty of time to read it in advance. Before the Christmas holidays, you see . . ." he said with the open, trusting face of the fool that he was.

NUMBED DOVER WAITS
FOR LISTS OF THE DEAD

There was a fine coat of snow over the Cliffs of Dover, making them whiter than ever over the weekend. The flag was at half-mast on Dover Castle, where the tourists go to stare across the Channel in happier times. The town, which has always claimed to be the largest passenger port in the world, had a heavy feel about it as the reality seemed to sink in.

One of the FEs was not coming home. There are eight of the Townsend Thoresen ships called *Free Enterprise*, and, just as Sealink vessels are known by affectionate nicknames or initials, the *Free Enterprises* were always the FEs, and they were always considered unsinkable.

All day long the local radio station broadcast the telephone numbers for inquiries, but stressed that there really wasn't very much more information. Anyone who had asked three hours ago need not try to ask again. The answer would be the same: they were trying to check the lists.

From Friday to Sunday, distraught relatives moved in a maddened circle from Dover to Maidstone, where the police headquarters had been set up, on to Gatwick, where some survivors had been flown in, then back to Dover, where thirty surviving crew members had returned unexpectedly on another ferry.

The horror of the first published lists was that nobody was utterly certain whether this was a list of known dead or known living. So to hear a name read from a list could have meant the best or the worst.

In Enterprise House, the company's Dover headquarters, the staff were red-eyed with lack of sleep and tears shed for friends and for the very fact of the catastrophe. In their blue uniforms, now looking crumpled and far from their usual jaunty image, they passed out coffee and beat away the onlookers and sightseers. Families sat in little clusters on the benches of the big departure hall; they followed the staff with their eyes and whenever a telephone rang on a desk, a small crowd would gather immediately, just in case.

Wearily, the ferry staff faced television teams and made statements. "I have been asked to say that the Kent Police will answer any questions from now on."

"Well, what have we all been doing here, for God's sake?" asked a man, distraught for news of his son. "I don't know. I'm terribly sorry, but we realize that the lists are incomplete. The Kent Police have sent a team to visit all the hospitals in Bruges to check the names again."

The man, whose face was so drawn it looked like a skull, clutched at her hand.

"If you do know, I'd prefer to hear it now. I don't want his mother to go on hoping." The tired girl from the ferries swore that she did not know. She pressed several tenpence pieces into his hand so that he could ring the police in Maidstone. "I'm sorry," she said again.

"I know you're sorry. He was only nineteen," the man said simply as he walked leadenly to the telephone.

On everyone's radio the announcer kept appealing for more money for the Disaster Fund. "The divers didn't give up out in that cold sea. Don't you give up on your contributions," he pleaded.

A woman who was waiting for her sister-in-law to come back from this continental shopping trip said that they might all be better off at home, looking at their televisions. There was no news to be gotten here. A Salvation Army woman gave her more tea and sat down beside her on the bench.

"Tell me about your sister-in-law. What did she go to buy?" she asked.

"She might be drowned." The woman was frightened to talk about her in case it might bring bad luck.

"But we don't know that. Tell me, what did she go to buy?"

"Well, she said there wasn't all that much in Zeebrugge and she would go on to this place called Knokke Heist that was nearby. What will happen to her children if she's gone?"

"Don't think about that yet. The Lord will help; tell me about this place where she went shopping. . . ."

Around the terminal building the crowds came and went, as if by looking at that cold, gray sea they could somehow make it more likely that people had been taken from it the previous Friday night. And all around the eastern dock there were the distressingly inappropriate advertisements saying that the Continent is nearer than you think, and, perhaps the saddest of all, the big signs, "They're here, the new big-value, luxury ferries."

It was the endless waiting that was so hard to watch, even as an outsider. People were passive and almost paralyzed in the never-never land of not being sure a full day and a half after the tragedy. Although every news bulletin gave statistics and numbers, coupled with pleas about not having false hopes that anyone could survive in the wrecked ship, there were still ambiguities about the names coming from Belgium and whether they were totally accurate.

Many relations had abandoned their posts and gone to the Continent to see for themselves. Others railed at the myth of efficient computers, which still couldn't tell you who had been on the ship and whether their names matched any lists of those alive in the hospital.

Gently, the police, the ferry officials, and clergymen explained that there had been such a panic, nobody was too sure of what names were given and what names were taken. These English-sounding names would be unfamiliar to Flemish and French speakers. These names were often not listed in the first place by the ferry people, since if you are allowed to take three passengers in your car, the names of everyone do not form part of the ship's bureaucracy.

And in the town that has so strenuously opposed the building of a Channel tunnel, people said that it would be a crime if this disaster were to lead to the public believing that a tunnel was the only way to cross the sea.

Quietly, and without the usual excitement and fuss of people going on their holidays, the passengers filed on and off the rows of ferryboats in the harbor. And in a wet, cold, sad Dover, the ships sailed in and out under the white cliffs. The seagulls called as they always did, but through the sleet and in the silence they seemed as sad as funeral bells.

LET'S TALK GRIDLOCK

When I went to live in London in the early 1970s I used to be knocked backward by the amount of traffic conversation that preceded every gathering. If you went to someone's house for dinner you were expected to give an account of how you hacked your way through the jungle to get there, as if the place were some kind of forest clearing in Borneo instead of a suburban house in Ealing, and in turn you had to listen to everyone else's story.

I decided it was a ritual, like the way a dog often turns around a lot before settling down: London people had to tell you where they left the M4 and how they had skirted around the back of Paddington. Then, when it had all been said, you could talk about real things.

It was very boring, and I used to thank the Lord that in Dublin there would never be endless traffic stories like this because there weren't a dozen alternative ways of getting from one place to another; you sort of went on the main road. So we could start the real conversation immediately, I thought. We were ahead of the game.

Wrong.

They're here.

And if you want to unleash them on yourself, just mention the three words "traffic management plan" and you'll get worse than you would believe possible.

And the really bad part about it is that there's no real solution except to leave three hours earlier than you need for everything, like in the middle of the night. And buy tapes with sounds of water rippling over little rocks, things that will calm you down, and keep saying, "ohm, ohm," and try to loosen your grip on the wheel if you see bones coming through white flesh on your knuckles.

That, and the knowledge that you are not alone, may help.

Listen to the conversations all around you: know that everyone else is in the same position. Get solidarity and comfort from realizing that the city has come to a standstill for everyone, not just for you. Listen, listen, and calm down.

In a restaurant, a couple waits for their host. He arrives at the door with a face like thunder, nearly taking the door of the restaurant, the waiter, and the people at two tables with him in his path to his own table. He starts dragging off his wet overcoat, his gloves: his face is purpling up by the moment.

"Jesus Christ" are the first words he gets out, and the place is treated to a description of how he waited for twenty minutes at one set of traffic lights, and ten at the next, and there was no parking and there were wardens and guards like spare parts at a wedding, walking around leering at people, and "Jesus Christ!" again bawled at the top of his voice.

The startled couple, who had been waiting for him for more than half an hour, lie and say they have been there for only five minutes: the crumbs of ten bread rolls prove them to be dishonest.

"Can I take your coat?" the waiter asks politely.

"Look, I don't need any hassle today, let me tell you."

The waiter moves nervously away: the man who owns the restaurant arrives to take the coat, which had been thrown half on a chair, half on the floor, with the gloves and a scarf, and the man looks as if he would kill anyone who tried to pat him down. "Out of my way," says the purple man in a choking voice that terrifies the wits out of his two lunch guests, who had wrongly thought they were going to have a nice meal out.

On the bus, the woman got up three times to ask the bus driver if there were any way he could go faster. The first two times he explained politely that there wasn't. The third time there was a slight edge to his voice when he asked had she any suggestions? Like maybe plowing through the solid line of traffic ahead of him? Or revving up seriously and taking the bus into a flight path ten feet above the line of trucks, cars, and buses below?

There were tears in her eyes.

"I'm sorry," she said, and went back to her seat.

People were kind and came up with suggestions. "Could she get off the bus and walk?"

No, she walked with a stick; she wouldn't be any quicker.

What about a taxi?

Wouldn't it be the same snail's pace?

Yes, but at least the taxi driver could take a different route. People will understand if you're late, they told her; everyone's late these days. It just can't be helped. Everyone understands.

The woman could not be consoled. It was an appointment with the bank. Everything depended on their getting this loan. The bank had a feeling that they had been unreliable in the past.

We all had the feeling that she might have been—the tears of mascara didn't make her look like a good risk.

The bus was silent, thinking about banks. Someone gave her a tissue and someone else loaned her a mobile phone. She made a poor job of explaining the traffic situation. None of us had any hope for the loan.

A boy stood at the bus stop—like everyone else he had been waiting forever as things went slowly by, grim-faced people from an adult world staring unhappily ahead. "Did you have a nice day at school?" asked an old lady anxious for a conversation—any conversation—to pass the time. The bus was two hundred yards away; it might take fifteen minutes to get to us.

"No," he said.

"Why was that, dear?"

"The bus was late getting there and the teacher asked how it was that the rest of the class got in, and I said they had fathers with cars and they all got up at six o'clock in the morning, and I was told not to give cheek."

"Yes, well," she said.

"And then we all got late to the football pitch because the bus didn't come, and there was no football, and now the bus hasn't come and I'm going to be late home and they're going to ask why I'm the only one late home, and none of them go out, but if I said that I'd be giving cheek again."

"It's a hard life," the old lady said.

"It's a shit life," said the boy, ending the friendship between them.

Outside a lawyer's office. An awkward meeting: two onetime friends have fallen out, a business is being wound up, there are still areas of disagreement about some outstanding debts.

"Let's try to get this done in as civilized a way as possible," says one of them.

"Yeah, well, it would be easier to be civilized if your bloody lawyer had turned up."

"He's stuck in traffic, his secretary said."

"Secretary? Gargoyle, more like. Where's she coming from, not letting us smoke in the building, for God's sake?"

They stood glumly in the rain smoking while traffic inched by.

Once they had cursed the traffic to the pit of hell, and counted the number of cars that had only one person each in them, there wasn't much to talk about. So they inhaled. And they talked about the old days, when they were starting out.

When the lawyer arrived yelping about gridlock and nobody caring and cities coming to a standstill, the two men were looking at each other as normal human beings. One of the few success stories of the Christmas traffic.

ENGAGED SIGNALS

On a sunny day this week there was a wedding. Quiet people, all of them. There were no hen parties with the bride being left tied to a lamppost, no stag parties with a stripper photographed in close contact with the groom. These were not the kind of people who would have a printed wedding list from which you picked a gift to buy for them. There were no "afters" where the young friends of the happy couple joined the wedding party for a disco. Nobody put any shaving foam on the car, or tied beer cans to the back of it.

The telegrams sent good wishes for future happiness rather than technical sexual advice. The best man told one clean joke about Saint Peter at the gate of heaven, which made everyone smile and nobody wince.

The photographer didn't spend hours and hours; there were no intrusive camcorders in the church. No excited pageboys and flower girls ran amok. There were no family arguments. There was no feeling that they had been hurried, ignored, or shortchanged by the hotel.

So, all right, what went wrong?

They did not invite someone who thought she was going to be invited. She was a neighbor and lifelong friend of the family; she is a little deaf now, and has to sit down rather than stand about during the sherry party. But then people *do* sit down, don't they? It couldn't be the reason they didn't invite her.

Could it? She has been over it all so many times, and it's so hard to know. She couldn't read any signals that would explain their attitude. She had known the bride since the girl was a little toddler and had been part of the whole wedding story, the steady line leading to the watch for Christmas and then the engagement ring. She had loved the whole romance unfolding, but she didn't make much of it, because young girls are so anxious at a time like this, it didn't do to look overeager.

She had even been in the house to help keep the conversation going when the groom's parents were brought over for an introduction some months back. She hadn't said much—she had stayed in the background—but they must have been pleased she was there to share the load of the evening.

Because she is on a pension and wouldn't be able to buy something grand enough, she polished up one of her own silver photograph frames and gave it as a wedding gift. It had been a wrench to part with it; it meant taking out a picture of her own parents, long dead. She had made light of the situation, handing it over with little fanfare. She had seen gifts from others as they arrived. It wasn't as if they were keeping quiet about it all in front of her. That's what made it so strange. She had behaved perfectly over it all, not being too curious about things and asking who gave this and who gave that.

She went to Dublin and bought an outfit. It was exhausting getting to the shops and carrying it all home again on the train. It was expensive, and took a bigger chunk of her savings than she had thought it would.

No, she hadn't shown it to the family, because you

didn't just presume; you waited to be asked. They would say, "You are coming, aren't you?" then you would say, "Heavens, no, you won't have room for the likes of me in the party," and then you accept. That's what would have happened.

Except there had been no invitation.

No, the bridal family didn't seem at all embarrassed about not having invited her; they had talked cheerfully about the wedding like you would talk about a bank holiday, something that everyone would share, except of course that she hadn't been invited to share it. She had tried not to show too much interest in case it looked like she was begging to be invited.

She cried in her bed for many nights and then decided that she wouldn't stay around to be humiliated, so she invented a friend who had invited her to stay. She booked a guesthouse that had the sole advantage of being near a railway station.

Now, someone who knew her, a person who to my mind is of a hugely endearing, interfering sort of nature, got to know about the situation, and a week before the wedding decided she would tell the wedding family of the terrible upset and wondered if there was a way they might discover a so-called mislaid invitation.

And then the other side of the coin was revealed. Their neighbor had made it totally clear she didn't want to go next to or near the wedding; she asked them nothing about their plans for the day and just nodded when they told her what they were going to do.

She hadn't bothered to get the couple a present but had just given them an old picture frame from her sideboard, not even wrapped, saying, "This will do you, won't it?"

She hadn't gotten an outfit or a single new thing to wear for it. She never asked where the young couple was going to live or what kind of things they had gotten to furnish their new home. She had come in to inspect the in-laws and sat there with gimlet eyes watching everything and saying nothing. When they tried to tell her about the seating plan and find out whom she'd like to be near she was shruggy and distant.

One evening it got too much for them; it was going to cost £26 a head for the guests. Why should they force her to come when she obviously didn't want to?

The bride's mother had a few second thoughts; maybe it was just her way, her manner, her style? But then she was forced to agree that people's way, manner, and style are actually how you know what they are like. We can't go around second-guessing everyone, analyzing them, wondering if they mean yes when they say no.

No, they said they hadn't been a bit cold to her themselves; they couldn't have done more to involve her.

The nice, interfering friend of whom I approve so heartily realizes much better than I do how you can't really rule the world and change the course of people's lives.

So she didn't play God.

And so on a sunny afternoon this week, a wedding took place without a neighbor and old friend, because the woman had sent out hostile and moody signals.

And a lonely woman sat in a bed-and-breakfast near a railway station and turned the pages of a magazine, her heart hard against a family who sent cold signals to her and had not managed to include her among the eighty guests who had given less valuable wedding gifts and bought less splendid wedding garments.

And because nobody ever thinks it's worthwhile to tell people that they really should show their affection and interest and not assume that everyone knows it's there: you can be quite sure the air around us is just humming with signals, all of which went the wrong way.

WHEN LITTLE LIES CAN
BE BIG MISTAKES

When some Americans were admiring the lovely soda bread in a house the other day, they said nobody made bread like the Irish. I waited for the woman who was serving it to tell them it was the stone-ground you buy in the supermarket and they could buy it at the airport on the way home. Then, with a roaring in my ears, I heard her say that it was nothing, she just threw in a handful of this and a handful of that like her grandmother had done.

And they all beamed at her and thought she was wonderful. I beamed at her and thought she was a liar.

A friend of ours set up as a smartish sort of dressmaker in London, she made velvet jackets for people and put her label in the back of them. She explained to me that jackets were a good way of advertising yourself, because people didn't usually take off their dresses or skirts at functions, and this was the only way people might see her name.

One of her more elegant friends removed the label in her jacket and put in a Harrods one instead. The friend thought it was an inverted compliment and the dressmaker thought she was a liar.

In a pub on Monday a couple were having a bank holiday drink and the bar owner asked them whom they were voting for. His daughter was a known supporter of Adi Roche as a candidate for the presidency.

The couple were loud in their support. Adi would surprise everyone; they knew dozens who were voting for her. The man behind the bar was pleased; he said he'd tell his daughter. It would give Adi a boost.

The couple left and got into their car, which had a rival's sticker. He saw them from the window. They thought they were being diplomatic; he thought they were a pair of liars.

At a book launch an author mentioned in passing a book she had written that none of us had read, or even heard of. She wasn't pausing to ask what we had thought of it or anything. There would be no interrogation on its subject matter.

Most of us gave a kind of lying murmur; there was a sort of mumble of words. "Oh, yes, yes indeed, I know, great success, marvelous idea. I remember it; that did very well. . . ." The kind of comfortable, noncommittal sort of wallpaper that we have all heard and nobody asks any questions.

One of the number, however, asked straight out what it was called, what it was about, how much it cost, and how it had done.

She thought the rest of us were liars; we thought she was being unnecessarily frank.

The woman was going to a wedding. Her ex-husband was going to be there with his new wife. She had what she called a New Look, and she was generally delighted with her outfit. But she lacked complete confidence, so she brought the hat along for a few impartial observers to see. It was very expensive and what she nervously described as a bit outlandish.

Now, I didn't see it because I wasn't one of her impartial observers, but I did see a picture of it. To my mind it was the hat for a jokey eighteen-year-old playing at being a glamour-puss. But seriously, what do I know? I just didn't like it for the wipe-their-eyes occasion for which it was intended.

So she asked the observers if they thought it was mutton dressed as lamb, or what. And although they didn't like it, they said they did. They said that she *felt* so good and young in it, it would have been counterproductive to say no. So they were false friends and liars or else supportive friends and kind people. One or the other. They told her it was great and she's wearing it.

The shop is untidy and badly managed and it's not any cheaper than anywhere else. It doesn't give credit or anything to attract that kind of customer. The place is a bit grubby, the staff not particularly helpful, and it's not doing well.

The couple who own it are beginning to say in stunned tones that they may have to sell out. They can't understand it. They are in such a good position; they were always told that the site was everything in terms of merchandising. It doesn't seem to be nowadays. They are bewildered by it.

The people in the town who like them and who still shop there and who are now getting this hard-luck story are behaving like liars. They say to the couple that business will surely pick up, that people tire of modern places,

and that old friends are the best friends. They say this because life is short and no shopkeepers could bear to hear
that their business is shabby and poorly kept and will
eventually and deservedly go down the tubes.

They are not liars, they say; they are kind people in a
small country town facing the fact that these shopkeepers
are not people who will be galvanized and motivated into
action by harsh if well-meant advice.

I have a friend whose mother-in-law always brings the
children licorice. As it happens, the children hate them.
The grandmother is not going to know this unless someone tells her, but the more little multicolored packets she
has delivered to false oohs and aahs of gratitude, the more
difficult it is to tell her.

This is the belief of the mother, who thinks that all children should learn to eat a little of everything and learn to
put up with what may well turn out to be a future of un-
wanted gifts and disappointments. It is not her eight-year-
old son's view. He says to her that she is telling Granny a
lie, that everyone spits them out as soon as they get out of
the room, and he asks why they can't tell her what they really want. She has to go into a sweetshop, hasn't she?
You're not meant to lie about other things, why about this?

Some friends went out for a meal last weekend. They
thought it was going to be an inexpensive night out, but by
the time everyone had ordered starters and desserts, and
waved away the notion of having the house carafe, it
turned out to cost a fortune.

For people who had expected to pay half that, it was a
huge disappointment. They did have inklings of how it
was turning out when they saw the prices on the menu.
But one villain said, "Oh, come on, let's go for it; let's treat

ourselves." The others ate and drank on, but full of resentment. And when the villain, who is basically good-natured, said, "Oh, dear, was that all too dear?" they decided they would be liars. No, they said, it was grand, lovely, well worth it.

True stories. I'd lie in three of them. Everyone else I asked said they'd lie in them all. Who can you trust nowadays?

CURMUDGEONS OF SUMMER

❧

"I don't like summer myself. Personally," said the girl in the pale pink shorts and the dark pink halter top. She was eating a huge ice-cream cone and waiting in the crowds to see the USS *JFK* come into view in Dun Laoghaire.

She looked like an advertisement for summer, with her shiny hair, her ninety-seven small, healthy teeth, her light suntan, and her air of well-being.

"I know," said her friend, who was no use as a friend. She had said, "I know," to people for all of her eighteen years, and you could tell she would do so forever. "I know what you mean."

The girl who didn't like summer, personally, was at least a person of views; she was prepared to elaborate on her stance.

"You see, the thing about summer is that you expect so much from it," she said earnestly. "Every time you open the papers or turn on the television there's someone saying, 'Here comes summer,' and you get all excited and then nothing much happens at all."

"Oh, I *know*," said the other one.

Socrates had a friend like that, didn't he, when he was writing the *Dialogues*, some dumbo who said, "Assuredly," every two pages or so.

Deeply depressing, I would have thought, and wouldn't have crossed the road to meet the guy again. But look at it this way; they remained mates, at least until the end of the book, so people might just appreciate that kind of attitude in other people. Anyway, the girl who didn't like summer, personally, seemed perfectly pleased with the response.

"Like they're always saying that the deep, dark days of winter are behind—I love winter."

"Oh, winter's great," said the other.

"And you could stay in bed on a winter morning without being demented by the birds, they've all gone down to the Mediterranean or died or something in winter; you'd get a bit of peace."

"The birds are brutal," said her friend.

"You know where you are in winter; you're cold and wet and you know that's what it's going to be; you haven't a clue where you are in summer."

"Not a clue."

"It could be pouring rain or roasting the skin off of you, and what's there to do anyway?"

"Tell me about it," said the other.

They were both gorgeous-looking, and getting many admiring looks from what I would have thought were fine, young, scantily dressed fellows.

"You know another thing about summer, you end up eating three hundred calories of this stuff without even realizing you're even doing it. . . ." said one.

The other one nodded until her head nearly fell off.

"You're right," she said. "You're too right."

I didn't wish the pink girl a more sunny attitude, or a

sense of priorities. I was sorry that she didn't have anyone
to disagree with her and to sing some song in praise of
summertime. I wished her a better friend.

The woman polishing her brasses was dying for a chat.
"It's a nightmare trying to keep the house right in summer," she said. I told her she was doing a great job of it.
But no, apparently the bright light of summer was the
enemy. You could shine and shine and some smear always
showed up. But the very worst thing was the way the bit of
brass polish comes off on the door. . . . Well, that kind of
thing goes unnoticed in winter, but at this time of the year
it's a nightmare.

I thought to myself that a nightmare was putting it a bit
strongly, and though a lot of people have very exacting
standards about housekeeping, there's a question of going
too far.

"You see, there should be some method, which means
that you only clean the brass and not the door," she said.
What I *should* have said, of course, was, "I know, this is
what you're up against." Why do I never realize that this is
the right thing to say almost all the time?

But I said that there was a woman who lived near us in
London who had little cardboard shields cut out, and she
used to lay them over the knocker and the letter box and
just clean within them so that the brass polish didn't get
on the door.

Well, if I had found the Holy Grail or the missing link,
she couldn't have been more interested. And was it heavy
cardboard, and did you stick it onto the door, or just hold
it, and imagine my doing that. She'd never have thought
it about me, just goes to show how wrong you can be
about people. She was going to go in and make one immediately, and would a cornflake box be strong enough,

or should it be something more sturdy, and what did I use myself?

I was purple in the face trying to tell her that I had never done it, but she didn't believe me. If you had a wonderful hint like that, then of course you'd use it. I had transformed her summer for her, she said. But don't you like summer anyway? I pleaded.

I wished she did, but in fact she didn't. The sofa covers faded, the net curtains looked grimy after three days, you realized how much of the place needed painting. One good thing about winter, she said mysteriously, was that everyone was in the same boat.

There's this couple who have been given the loan of a mobile home for a week. They were delighted because they thought they could have one last real family holiday before the kids grew up and wanted to go off on their own. There's only one problem. The children think they *are* grown-up and have planned to go off on their own already. They're fifteen and sixteen, for heaven's sake. What would they be doing going on a holiday with their parents?

A holiday is what it says it is; it's time off to enjoy yourself, to be free to do what you want. The mobile home would be like home, but even more uncomfortable. You'd have to be in for meals and clear up after them, and you wouldn't be allowed to go anywhere.

No, they don't quite say it like this, but that's the drift.

And they don't buy the idea of it being one last holiday either. You can be absolutely certain that come next year there'll be one more "last holiday," and so on until they are old and gray.

The kind thing to do is to cut it now and let the parents realize that it's not about packing Scrabble and a family-size NIVEA Creme anymore.

I know I'm a softy, but I wish there could have been a compromise. That the children could have come to the mobile home for just a weekend. That way things wouldn't have looked so bleak for good, warm people whose only crime was to want to enjoy the summer.

DON'T SHOOT

⌒

The woman who was dealing angrily with her face in the ladies' room had a determined sort of look. Whatever unappealing thing she seemed to find in the environs of her nose would be dealt with, and stay dealt with.

There was serious grouting and in-filling being done there. I looked at her handbag with interest to discover how many tools she had brought with her for this purpose. This kind of massive overhaul job was usually done, I thought, back at base.

And there, inside the rim of her handbag, was a long piece of beige linen, and embroidered on it in red were the words "Don't Kill the Messenger."

It's what urban myths are made of. Next I would see an ax and discover she went around dabbing at her nose and hacking people to death all over the city.

I looked at the exit and worked out that my chances of making it were not great. My only hope was to outwit her and pretend I hadn't seen the message. I scrubbed at my hands furiously with the soap and tried to saunter to the door.

"You probably wonder what that means," she said.

"No, not at all," I said in a squeak, realizing too late that I should have seen nothing at all to wonder about. I'd have been no good in intelligence.

"My children gave it to me on my birthday. It was meant to be a joke—a joke that should be taken seriously."

"Well, now," I said.

"I have a habit of sounding off when something happens, you see," she confessed.

"Well, don't we all?" I tried not to let my fevered imagination wonder how violently she had sounded off and what had to happen to make her do so. It couldn't be *too* bad if her children had made a joke of it and embroidered a sampler for her.

She said it had been a great shock; they had given her flowers, of course, and other things, but her three children decided that this would be the most practical and helpful thing they could give her: a little reminder for Mother's handbag. Because whenever she had been about to kill the messenger, it appeared that her handbag would be open or she would be on the point of opening it.

And what kinds of messengers had she killed?

She would like to know that, too, she told me; she would very much like to know, and then she had asked for incidents that could have led to such an accusation. They had been very sparse and would not have stood up in a court of law.

Anything at all specific?

Oh, the time she had spoken her mind to the man in the DART office about the poor timetable. Her daughters had taken a bad view about that. They said that he wasn't personally responsible, and that Mother should have written to the authorities or organized a letter of protest from the neighborhood, or written to a newspaper or a radio program about it.

She hadn't really meant to attack *him*, of course, but he was there, and he did represent the people who ran the DART, so he might have expected a little ill will to be vented now and then when shortcomings were noticed, and surely he would pass this to the proper people? Her daughters didn't think so.

And her son was put out because she spoke sharply to a man on a garage forecourt about some negative aspects of the Shell Corporation in Nigeria.

She said that the whole thing had been exaggerated beyond all imaginings. And it was quite irresponsible to compare her to those all-powerful army generals in the past who killed the messenger when he brought bad news of an army defeat.

That's what the allusion was, she said cuttingly; she was being cast in the role of someone who just lashed out at the first and usually least responsible member of the team that committed the outrage.

"It's very easy to do," murmured Maeve the peacemaker.

I told her that I used to attack the air hostesses about unexplained noises in the soft underbellies of jumbo jets and blame them because the pilots used to begin every announcement with a great strangled growl of "aaaarrgh." It's only a mannerism, a sort of preparatory throat clearing, but to those with a slightly nervous disposition it sounds as if they are being held firmly at the neck by a hijacker with a smoking grenade. Only when an air hostess told me kindly that she really could not go into the flight deck and correct the captain's diction did I realize I was attacking the nearest target.

I thought this nice, humble, and honest admission would help the ruffled mother and make her feel that she was not alone, that if I had three children they might have embroidered the same thing for me.

But she was accepting no consolation. She had been in a supermarket recently where they had changed everything around; she found herself looking at stir-fry sauces where once they had all the teas and coffees. Who *else* should she attack other than the girl stacking the shelves?

The family had been very annoyed when she reported that incident. And the one involving the taxi driver who was late because the firm had not contacted him in time and he had to come miles from a taxi rank, and the waiter in the restaurant where the smoking tables were too far away from the buzzy part.

Her view was that there simply wasn't *time* to write to the heads of supermarkets, owners of restaurants, managers of taxi firms, and certainly not enough time to wait to get on the talk shows, and suppose you *did* get on those shows; you might run the risk of being considered a crank.

We had both said how we didn't like those hot-air things for drying your hands. She believed they gave you warts; I believe they are deafening and don't really dry your hands—paper towels are much better.

At that moment a woman came in to clean the cloakroom. I could see the ruffled mother's mouth open. She was just about to blame the cleaner.

I tapped her handbag in a warning manner. Together we wrote a postcard to the hotel manager, courteously expressing our dissatisfaction with the hand-drying operation. I have received a reply already and I'm sure she has, too. Not entirely convincing, it says that they're high on being antigerm, incapable of giving you warts, and not at all deafening for the majority of customers.

Like they did a survey since, maybe?

But still, it's a start.

I saved the girl who cleaned the taps from an ear bash-

ing, and maybe after the polite letter about the drying machine that breaks through the threshold of pain in terms of
noise the manager might pay a courtesy visit to the ladies'
room and listen to it. And I have learned that crisis inter-
vention in terms of embroidering any little maxims of life
is not a great idea.

Whatever the temptation, and no one on earth is more
perpetually tempted than myself to tell people how to run
their lives, we *must* remember not only does this hurt people to the quick, it also turns out to be useless.

FLASHES OF INSIGHT
IN THE SUN

⌒

This woman was very bored with me. She had hoped to meet someone far more glittery at the do, and she seemed stuck with me for the next five minutes.

She ran a dress shop. I said it must be hard to know what people would like and stock the right things. She looked at me and said no, it wasn't hard at all. Because I am eager that even the most casual conversations should go pleasantly rather than be filled with fury, I said that was wonderful, and it was probably because she knew her customers well and could guess their tastes. She said no, she didn't know them at all; she got passing trade and she just stocked things that looked good, and would sell.

She yawned a terrible yawn in my face.

With the best will in the world I couldn't think of much to say to that, so I said, "aah," meaningfully, and wondered why I could not just be silent, as most of the world is when faced with things like that. So I *was* silent for a bit—smiling, of course, but wordless.

She said the woman who just came in had once been a man, and was now a perfect size ten and looked great in Versace, and the twins who looked like Lady This and

Lady That were actually on the game and worked to-gether. You had to have both of them or neither of them, and they made a fortune. She said her own ex-husband was at the party and she was interested to see he had re-moved his gold watch and put it in his pocket when he had noticed her there—he didn't want it to be thought he had any assets left.

She had quite cheered up now and decided she would bring me out of myself. "It must be frightfully hard to think of things to write about," she said sympathetically. "I mean, life is pretty dull, isn't it?"

Grateful acknowledgment is made to the following
for permission to reprint previously published material:

Irish Times: Brief excerpt from a letter dated February 19, 2004,
from Tony Allwright. Reprinted by permission of the *Irish Times*.
Random House, Inc.: Excerpt from *The Dyer's Hand and Other Essays*
by W. H. Auden, copyright © 1948, 1950, 1952, 1953, 1954, 1956, 1957, 1958, 1960,
1962 by W. H. Auden. Reprinted by permission of Random House, Inc.